W9-BXW-769

SELF-DEVELOPMENT FOR SUCCESS

Stress management

Acknowledgements

The author wishes to thank the
following people for their help
in writing this book:
Consultants of MaST
International Organization plc
for their help with the text, and
Heather Barker for reading and
typing the text.

SELF-DEVELOPMENT FOR SUCCESS

Stress management

THE ESSENTIAL GUIDE TO THINKING AND WORKING SMARTER

Gerard Hargreaves

AMERICAN MANAGEMENT ASSOCIATION

AMACOM
American Management Association
New York • Atlanta • Boston • Chicago • Kansas City
San Francisco • Washington, D. C.
Brussels • Mexico City • Tokyo • Toronto

A Marshall Edition
Conceived, edited, and designed by
Marshall Editions Ltd.
The Orangery, 161 New Bond Street
London W1Y 9PA

This book is available at a special discount when ordered in bulk quantities. For information, contact Special Sales Department, AMACOM, an imprint of AMA Publications, a division of American Management Association,1601 Broadway, New York, NY 10019.

This publication is designed to provide accurate and authoritative information in regard to the subject matter covered. It is sold with the understanding that the publisher is not engaged in rendering legal, accounting, or other professional service. If legal advice or other expert assistance is required, the services of a competent professional person should be sought.

Library of Congress Cataloging–in–Publication Data
Hargreaves, Gerard
    Stress management / Gerard Hargreaves.
        p.   cm
    Includes biographical references and index.
    ISBN 0-8144-7022-X
    1. Stress (Pschology). 2. Stress management   I Title.
BF575.S75H395 1999
155.9'042--dc21   98-53810
                                                        CIP

Printing number

10 9 8 7 6 5 4 3 2 1

Series Consultant Editor Chris Roebuck
Project Editor Jo Wells at Axis Design
Designer Sandra Marques at Axis Design
Indexer Livia Vass at Axis Design
Art Director Sean Keogh
Managing Art Editor Patrick Carpenter
Managing Editor Clare Currie
Editorial Assistant Sophie Sandy
Editorial Coordinator Rebecca Clunes
Production Nikki Ingram

Cover photography Tony Stone Images

Originated in Italy by Articolor
Printed and bound in Portugal by Printer Portuguesa

Contents

1

The Body
The Mind
Performance
Symptoms

What is stress?

How does stress affect performance?

What are the early warning signs?

What is Stress?

With enough pressure to match your ability to cope you can live a healthy and happy life. Too much pressure and you may suffer from stress-related illnesses. Too little pressure may also result in stress. Feelings of boredom, worthlessness, or lack of self-esteem all can induce stress.

Stress is a normal part of everyday life. When managed well, it can work in a positive way to help you to perform better. But badly managed, or ignored, it can be a killer. Stress is the body's response to the demands placed on it. The amount of pressure will determine whether you can cope or not.

Stress questionnaires appear in magazines and newspapers regularly, and many businesses conduct stress management courses. There is no doubt that stress-related illnesses are on the increase. Grievance committees and courts are seeing a growth in the number of cases appearing before them whose root causes are stress.

The word "stress" comes from the Latin word *stringere,* which means hardship. The word "stress," as we use it now, is an abbreviated form of "distress."

The psychologist Hans Selye, who contributed much to our understanding of stress with his work in the seventies, was one of the first to use the term "stress" to denote a potentially damaging force. He also spoke of a "state of stress" to describe bodily changes in response to a stressful situation.

Stress management is an issue of managing the demands and pressures placed on you, in the most effective way. The point at which positive pressure turns into negative stress varies for each individual. It will also vary at different times in your life. This changing pattern presents another challenge as you attempt to manage your stress.

Stress and control

The diagram (bottom left) can help you understand how choice and control are vital elements in the experience of stress.

Area 1: Chosen high arousal
A challenging situation that you have chosen – a demanding but rewarding job – can cause moderate stress.

Area 2: Imposed high arousal
Experiencing pressure but little control, such as tight deadlines or long hours at work, creates stress.

Area 3: Imposed low arousal
If you have little to do and little control – you find yourself unemployed – the result may be stress.

Area 4: Chosen low arousal
A situation in which you have little to do by choice will produce little stress.

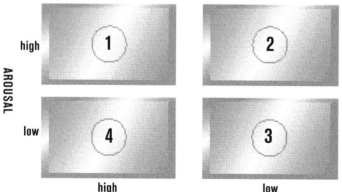

AROUSAL — high / low

CHOICE — high / low

1   2
4   3

The Cost of Stress

There are many figures available on the cost of stress to individuals, employers, and the government. They all present a picture of an increased trend towards stress-related illnesses and the resulting increase in associated financial costs.

Measurable stress

Stress in the workplace costs ten times more than industrial disputes. As estimated by the National Safety Council, a million employees are absent on an average workday. In addition, 75–90 percent of visits to primary care physicians are stress related. Stress costs the American industry $200–300 billion annually. Stress is expensive! These figures show only what is measurable. Yet, this is far from the full picture.

Non-measurable stress

Some costs of stress are difficult to measure. How can you put a price on the reduction of productivity at work due to stress or to the potential lost income due to reduced creativity?

Industrial illness

Stress is now recognized as a bonafide illness, and several compensation claims have been awarded. One example of compensation for stress was an award to a social worker employed by a county council. The department had undergone reorganization, which resulted in an increased volume of work for the social worker who brought the case. This, in turn, created stress and anxiety which eventually led to a nervous breakdown. The social worker promised additional support by the employer – when this did not materialize, he began to suffer further stress symptoms. After a second nervous breakdown this employee had no option but to retire early. The judge in the case held that the council was liable for its employee's second breakdown and awarded substantial damages to the social worker.

MEASURABLE COSTS OF STRESS
- Sickness
- Early retirement
- Death at work
- Accidents/injury
- Absenteeism
- Health care costs

NON-MEASURABLE COSTS OF STRESS
- Slow/poor performance
- Poor time management
- Bad decision-making
- Ineffective management
- Prone to accidents
- Conflicts in interpersonal relationships
- Lack of concentration
- Impaired judgement
- Reduced creativity

The Stress Balance

We usually associate stress with having too many pressures. For example, a high-pressure job, having to make lots of decisions, or bringing up and supporting a family are familiar sources of stress. There are, however, times when we do not have enough demands and pressures put on us; and life can become unfulfilling and stressful in a different way.

The point at which demands become too much for a person to cope with will vary greatly among individuals.

Too many demands cause stress

If demands are higher than your ability to cope, you will suffer from the negative effects of stress. At various points in your life the demands upon you can increase. For example, if your job changes or you start a family, this may produce new challenges which are difficult to adjust to.

Too few demands cause stress

When demands fall below a certain level, but your ability to cope stays the same, you may suffer the negative effects of stress, such as boredom or insecurity. For example, you may suffer stress while recovering from an illness because you are unable to get on with your normal life. Retirement can be another source of stress. If you are used to having a great deal of stimulation in your day-to-day work life, the sudden reduction in activity can be a stressor. A repetitive and undemanding job can also be a cause of stress, as well as considerable frustration and anxiety.

Stress balance

When demands on you are equal to your ability to cope, you will manage the stress in your life effectively and remain in control.

TOO MUCH STRESS   **STRESS AND COPING IN BALANCE**   **TOO LITTLE STRESS**

Case Study

John and Jean are a couple in their mid-30s with three young children. John is a junior manager in a large factory. They have been finding the cost of bringing up young children challenging, and Jean has decided to take an evening job. A new regime has begun in their household, and John finds that it has increased his stress levels, even by the end of the first day.

John now has to be home from work at 6:00 p.m. to supervise the children's evening meal, homework, bath, and bed time. During the day he is intensely aware of his responsibilities and organizes his work around them. He becomes very tense when a meeting runs late. At quitting time, his colleagues are surprised to see him leave on time, because he usually works late. He feels embarrassed when he bumps into his boss on his way out.

Despite delays on his trip home, John manages to get home at exactly 6:00 p.m. by walking most of the way. Jean is able to leave for work on time.

John has been looking forward to watching a football game on TV and has planned the rest of his evening around it. But he has to cope with one problem after another. The two-year-old has his bath but won't go to sleep. The ten-year-old refuses to do her homework. She eventually finishes it and offers to bathe the five-year-old. John quickly starts the dishes, thinking that he will still have plenty of time to watch the football game, but the five-year-old starts crying because she has soap in her eyes. John loses his temper and shouts at the children. The older girl storms off, sulking, and the two-year-old starts crying again.

By the time the children are all in bed, John has five minutes left to do the dishes. He finally sits down in front of the TV at 9:30 p.m. Ten minutes later he is asleep. Jean wakes him when she returns at 10:00 p.m. When she asks how his evening went, even though he feels grumpy, tired and resentful, he tells her that everything is fine.

How could John cope better?

He could increase the resources available to help him out, perhaps by buying a dishwasher or a VCR. It may be possible to change his work schedule, perhaps by working flextime. It may be also be possible to change the existing routine. Do all of the children need a bath every night? Rushing around the house only created more tension in the children. Could he learn to relax more? The rush to finish by 9:00 p.m. placed extra pressure on the family. He should avoid setting unrealistic deadlines. Sharing his real feelings with his wife would be healthier than "stuffing" them.

JOHN'S SOURCES OF STRESS AT WORK

- Having to leave work on time
- Greater pressure to finish his tasks at work
- Teasing from his colleagues when he leaves on time
- Worries about the perception of his superiors regarding his commitment
- No room for delays on his journey home

JOHN'S SOURCES OF STRESS AT HOME

- A new set of skills to master
- A rigid pattern with difficult deadlines
- Dealing with unforeseen demands from the children

The Human Performance Curve

Cardiologist Dr. Peter Nixen's *Human Performance Curve* helps to understand the effects of stress on your ability to perform everyday roles and responsibilities. The curve shows how performance in a given situation rises with increased arousal (stimulation).

Changing stress levels

The left-hand side of the curve shows positive arousal and healthy performance. Generally, someone on this side of the curve will be managing the pressures and demands of life and enjoying a balanced lifestyle. They will probably feel alert, relaxed, confident, and energetic. Performance is enhanced by this "balanced lifestyle."

However, if demands increase and undermine this healthy lifestyle, the person will be pushed to the right-hand side of the curve. If steps are not taken to manage these extra demands, they could potentially cause long-term damage. If the extra demands are recognized and positive actions are taken, the person will continue to manage successfully and remain healthy.

Optimum performance occurs when you are effectively and positively able to manage all the demands with which you are are confronted by life.

People get pushed over the top of the curve, often without realizing it, when they get so involved in aspects of their

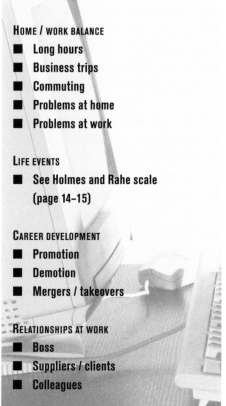

COMMON SOURCES OF DEMANDS

HOME / WORK BALANCE
- Long hours
- Business trips
- Commuting
- Problems at home
- Problems at work

LIFE EVENTS
- See Holmes and Rahe scale (page 14–15)

CAREER DEVELOPMENT
- Promotion
- Demotion
- Mergers / takeovers

RELATIONSHIPS AT WORK
- Boss
- Suppliers / clients
- Colleagues

job, families, or hobbies that they fail to take a step back and allow time to rest and recharge their batteries. They continue to take on burdens without realizing the damage they are doing to themselves until it is too late. At this point, the smallest event may push them over the top. It may be something relatively insignificant in itself, such as a machine breaking down or an argument with someone at work.

Listen to your body

Awareness of the possible effects of what is happening in your life is the key to beginning to manage your stress. Listen to what your body is telling you. If you start to get headaches, don't just take a few pills and hope they will go away. Ask yourself what is happening in your life, which is causing you to have the headaches. Recognize the causes of stress, and take steps to address them. When you have been under pressure and you feel yourself on the downward slope, take steps to reduce fatigue.

Stress, the family and work

It is important to recognize the impact of stress on the family as a whole. If your family has already been coping with a difficult situation, such as a major illness or moving to a new house, now may not be the best time to embark on a major redecorating program which will cause further upheaval. The same principles apply to your team at work. If the team is to maintain a high performance level, it will need time to recover after working towards a major deadline and putting in long hours.

ASK YOURSELF THE FOLLOWING QUESTIONS:
Am I on the downward slope?
Is too much being demanded of me?
Am I in control?
Is my performance being affected because I am too angry or tense?
Am I sleeping well?
Am I keeping myself fit enough to cope?

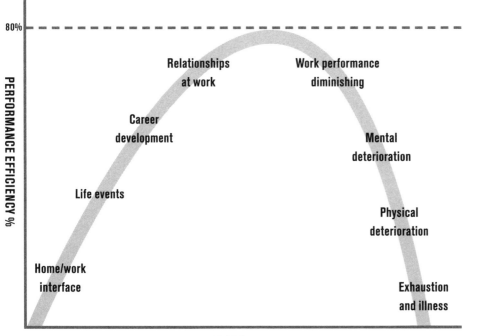

80%

PERFORMANCE EFFICIENCY %

Relationships at work

Work performance diminishing

Career development

Mental deterioration

Life events

Physical deterioration

Home/work interface

Exhaustion and illness

AROUSAL

The Life Change Index

The table below is adapted from Holmes and Rahe's *Life Change Index*. The index allocates a score to the major stress-inducing events in life. Tick all those that have happened to you in the last 12 months, and add them up. Your total score will indicate how likely you are to suffer from a stress-related illness in the near future.

Everyone is different

Of course, the amount of stress each life event will produce varies from person to person. The effect of different events will also vary among cultures. For example, attitudes toward the role of marriage and divorce may differ greatly; this can have an impact on how stressful either will be perceived by an individual. Your

Life Event	Mean Value		Life Event	Mean Value	
Death of spouse	100		Son or daughter leaving home	29	
Divorce	73		Trouble with in-laws	29	
Marital separation	65		Spouse begins or stops work	28	
Jail term	63		Outstanding personal achievement	26	
Death of close family member	63		Beginning or ending school	26	
Personal injury or illness	53		Change in living conditions	25	
Marriage	50		Revision of personal habits	24	
Being fired	47		Trouble with boss	23	
Marital reconciliation	45		Change in work hours		
Retirement	45		or conditions	20	
Change in health of family member	44		Change in residence	20	
Pregnancy	40		Change in schools	20	
Sexual difficulties	39		Change in recreation activities	19	
Gaining a new family member	39		Change in church activities	18	
Business readjustment	39		Change in social activities	18	
Change in financial status	38		Change in sleeping habits	16	
Death of close friend	37		Change in number of family		
Change to different line of work	36		get-togethers	15	
More arguments with spouse	35		Change in eating habits	15	
High mortgage	31		Vacation	13	
Foreclosure of mortgage or loan	30		Christmas	12	
Change in responsibilities at work	29		Minor violations of the law	11	

particular situation, belief system, and the general state of your health will also have an impact upon the extent to which life events tend to affect you.

Manage your stress

The scale highlights the need to be aware of what is happening in your life and to manage your stress effectively. When new events create additional sources of stress, perhaps you should reassess your life and areas in which you can reduce the pressures you are feeling.

For example, if you have changed jobs, moved to a new house, increased your mortgage – and your children have started attending a new school during the same short period – it may be a good idea to reduce your social or work-related responsibilities. Perhaps you could resign as secretary of the sports club or cut down on working long hours.

Obviously, it would be preferable to wait a few months, until you have had a chance to adapt to the new changes in your life and are feeling more relaxed about them, before you attempt to take on any new challenges.

What does your score mean?

0–149

Everyone has a 10 percent chance of developing a stress-related illness in the next two years.

150–199

You are 40 percent more likely than normal to develop a stress-related illness in the next two years.

Perhaps there have been extra demands putting pressure on you lately. Try and relax more and to manage some of those stressful events more effectively.

200–299

You are 50 percent more likely than normal to develop a stress-related illness in the next two years. Life has obviously been very hectic lately.

More than 300

You are 80 percent more likely than normal to develop a stress-related illness in the next two years. Stop! Look at what is happening in your life and take action to reduce your stress level.

If you feel upset, ask yourself these questions: What am I telling myself that is making me feel this way? What is the expectation I have that is being challenged in this situation? Am I demanding that I should be treated in a particular way? Am I blaming another person for disturbing my peace of mind, when really it is only my judgement that is disturbing me? What is really being threatened?

Your Body And Stress

Any stressful event or activity, whether positive or negative, causes a physiological response in your body. As the performance curve shows, when managed effectively, this response can energize you to perform well. When it is not managed well, it can cause damage to your body.

There are two branches within the central nervous system that affect the response to stress: the sympathetic and the parasympathetic nervous systems.

The sympathetic nervous system

When you perceive a threat or a challenge, the sympathetic nervous system is activated. This is often referred to as the "fight-or-flight" response. The brain receives a message about the situation, which activates the pituitary gland. This, in turn, activates the adrenal glands to produce adrenaline. A chain reaction occurs (opposite page).

The responses of the sympathetic nervous system can give rise to physical stress indicators, such as:

- palpitations
- hyperventilation
- stomach problems
- sweaty palms
- muscle spasms
- cold feet and hands

	Response	Effect
Stage 1	RED ALERT! Body and brain prepare for action. Increase in supply of oxygen to the muscles and brain. This provides energy for action and heightens decision making in the short term. Pupils are enlarged to improve visual sensitivity.	Respond to danger: ■ Meet it, and return to equilibrium. ■ Fail to meet it, and the damaging effects continue.
Stage 2	Blood vessels to nonessential organs, such as skin and digestive system, are constricted. Liver releases glucose into the blood. The liver, skin, and digestive system release fatty acids into the blood. These provide extra energy.	Unless excess fats are used up, they will damage the body.
Stage 3	Exhaustion because the body has used up all its energy stores.	Serious illness and possibly death.

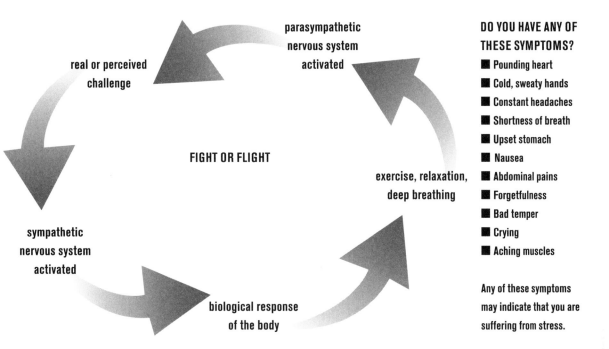

parasympathetic
nervous system
activated

real or perceived
challenge

FIGHT OR FLIGHT

exercise, relaxation,
deep breathing

sympathetic
nervous system
activated

biological response
of the body

DO YOU HAVE ANY OF THESE SYMPTOMS?
- Pounding heart
- Cold, sweaty hands
- Constant headaches
- Shortness of breath
- Upset stomach
- Nausea
- Abdominal pains
- Forgetfulness
- Bad temper
- Crying
- Aching muscles

Any of these symptoms may indicate that you are suffering from stress.

The parasympathetic nervous system

The general wellbeing of the body – rest, relaxation, food, the digestive process, and tissue repair – is governed by the parasympathetic nervous system. Unlike the sympathetic nervous system, the parasympathetic nervous system is not self-activating. You must consciously switch it on. Hence the need for deep breathing, positive thinking, and relaxation.

On a day-to-day basis, the body fluctuates between the responses of the two nervous systems to maintain a balance. When something dramatic happens, the balance is upset.

Long-term stress

In addition to the body responding immediately to unexpected or unusual life events, it can also suffer stress as a result of a buildup in demands and lifestyle changes over a much longer period of time. This is known as chronic, or the "drip-drip," stress.

Sources of this type of stress might include many years of commuting or feeling trapped in an unsatisfactory job or relationship. Episodic and long-term stress can be damaging, and both require effective and immediate management in order to prevent them from adversely affecting your health.

The Mind And Stress

The mind responds to the demands and pressures of life and exhibits its own symptoms of stress. For example, you have probably been aware of your mind's response to stress if you have lain awake at night worrying about the day ahead, perhaps before an interview, meeting, or important exam.

Worry can quite quickly get out of control, and you may find that your own negative thoughts become another source of stress.

COMMON STRESS-CREATING "MUSTS"

- I must always be on time.
- Other people must always be on time.
- I must visit my relatives every Sunday.
  (If you are bad-tempered and resentful when you arrive, no-one will enjoy the visit.)
- We must meet every Monday evening.
  (Is there any point in meeting if you have nothing to discuss?)
- I must always say "yes" when asked to do additional work or stay late.
  (Other commitments such as family events must be given an appropriate level of priority.)
- I must earn a high salary to afford the large house and expensive car.
  (Do material benefits matter more than your health?)
- I must get on with everybody.
- I must always be there for others in their hour of need.
  (Your own needs are just as important as those of other people.)

Some common mental symptoms of stress are:

- depression
- muddled thinking
- loss of sleep
- negative thoughts
- crying
- overreacting
- worrying unnecessarily
- moodiness

General attitudes and stress

As well as worrying about individual events, the general way you think about yourself and your lot in life can be a cause of stress. Many people cause themselves unnecessary worry because they (and those around them) do not match up to unrealistic, self-imposed beliefs or conditions.

You will create a lot of stress for yourself and others if you build many "musts" and "shoulds" into your life. When these beliefs are considered closely, they rarely create a genuine case of "must." More often, it is a case of "could like to" or "try hard to."

Do you recognize any of these unrealistic beliefs?

"I should be good at everything."
"You are what you are, and it is not possible to change."
"There is an answer to all of life's problems, I just need to find it."

MIND GAMES

Your own mind can play games with you which increase your stress levels. When you are under pressure and finding it difficult to cope with life's demands, it is easy to see everything negatively.

- **All or nothing thinking**
  It is not realistic to believe that you are either a total success or a total failure.
- **Discounting the positive**
  It is not helpful to dwell on the negatives and think that positive achievements don't count.
- **Catastrophizing**
  Avoid assuming the worst possible outcome to even the most insignificant events.
- **Labelling**
  It is common to identify with your shortcomings, telling yourself, "I am an idiot," rather than saying, "I made a mistake; let's move on."
- **Personalizing and blaming**
  It is unrealistic and useless to always blame yourself. For example, "If I hadn't left the chair there, he wouldn't have walked into it."

Think again

Must you do all of the things you believe you should? Yes, it is good business practice to plan and organize yourself to be on time for meetings and appointments, but you cannot be responsible for a traffic jam or the cancellation of a train. It is better to arrive a few minutes late, relaxed and able to function effectively, than tense, worked up, and with a headache.

Think of the "musts," "shoulds," and "mights" that govern your life. Try and change the way you think about them.

Instead of thinking, "I must be on time," try to think, "I am going to plan and organize myself so that I am on time." If circumstances beyond your control prevent you being on time, try not to panic, get angry, or worry. Instead, take control of the situation. In practical terms this may mean that, as soon as you can, make a phone call to let the people who are expecting you know that you will be delayed. In mental terms this will mean taking control of your responses and calming down so that when you do arrive you are not flustered and upset.

Early Warning Signs

The following tables give lists of common symptoms of stress. They are divided into the four areas of your life in which they tend to be manifested – physical, emotional, mental, and behavioral. As your personal level of stress increases, more of these symptoms are likely to become apparent. Perhaps you routinely exhibit a few of them whenever you are not coping well with the demands that life is placing upon you. For example, you may find that you often develop a rash, lose your appetite, feel queasy, or have difficulty sleeping when you feel anxious. Although the symptoms are often inconvenient and uncomfortable, they act as invaluable alarm signals, alerting you to the strain you are placing on your body and mind. Being able to identify your own personal indicators will help you to take early action and thus prevent your stress levels from getting out of control.

Physical Signs		Emotional Signs	
1	Headaches often increase in frequency and intensity when you are under pressure.	1	Feeling irritable and short-tempered usually indicates that you are feeling under pressure.
2	Muscle tension, most commonly in the head, neck, shoulders, and back can be an early warning sign.	2	Depression and a general feeling of gloom can result from stress that affects your general outlook on life.
3	The skin is particularly sensitive to stress. Dry skin, spots, and irritation are all classic reaction symptoms.	3	Loss of confidence and self-esteem can result from the feeling of being out of control when the demands upon you outweigh your ability to cope.
4	Digestive problems, such as an upset stomach, indigestion, or the development of an ulcer can be a warning sign that you are not coping well with stress.	4	If you are feeling drained and lacking in enthusiasm, this may stem from feeling overwhelmed.
5	Heart palpitations and chest pains can often be stress related.	5	A sense of alienation can result from an inability to cope.

How many of the symptoms listed in the tables below are you experiencing, either continuously or just from time to time? You may not have realized that some of the symptoms, such as feeling restless, can also be the result of stress.

Even though some of your symptoms may have a clear physical cause, such as indigestion due to bad eating habits or headaches caused by a badly lit office, count them nevertheless. They are likely to be an indirect consequence of stress.

ACT NOW

- Awareness is more than half the battle against stress.
- Think carefully about all aspects of your life.
- Recognize the symptoms and causes of stress.
- Take action to cut out the causes, and minimize the effects of tension around you.

Mental Signs		Behavioural Signs	
1	Lack of concentration is often a symptom of having too many things going round and round in your head.	1	Disturbed sleep patterns, whether insomnia or an increased need for sleep, are a sure sign that you are feeling stressed.
2	Indecision, even about trivial matters, is a classic symptom of stress.	2	Drinking and smoking more than usual are often attempts to find short-term stress relief.
3	Memory can be adversely affected by stress. You may find that you forget facts and figures, or the names of people and places you would usually remember.	3	A reduced sex drive is a common symptom of stress. It can often increase your worries and anxiety and cause you to withdraw from a supportive relationship.
4	Stress impairs judgement, leading to bad decision-making and mistakes.	4	Withdrawal from the company of friends and family or office relationships usually means that you are feeling unable to cope.
5	Persistently negative thoughts about yourself or your situation is probably a sign that you are not coping well with the demands placed upon you. This will make you feel even worse.	5	If you find it difficult to relax and are often fidgeting and unable to sit still, you are probably under stress.

2

Questions
Answers
Scores
Assessment

How do I perform?

Does my lifestyle cause stress?

Is my job stressful?

Lifestyle and Stress

The way you live your life is a key factor in determining your vulnerability to stress. Today, it is generally understood that lifestyle has a considerable impact on stress level. The contributory factors are: your attitude towards yourself; how you treat other people; the type of work you do; how you go about your day-to-day life; and whether or not you exercise, take time to relax, and eat properly. All of these factors will have a strong influence on how well you cope with the demands placed upon you and the likelihood of suffering from stress.

BE BRUTALLY HONEST WITH YOURSELF – ARE ANY OF THE FOLLOWING TRUE FOR YOU?

- ■ I regularly work more than five days a week.
- ■ I regularly work long hours.
- ■ I rush meal times.
- ■ I feel frustrated with my job.
- ■ I have no time for hobbies or fun things.
- ■ I don't exercise regularly.
- ■ I don't sleep well at night or can't get enough sleep.
- ■ I think relaxing is a waste of time.
- ■ I am short-tempered with people around me.

If you have answered "yes" to any of these, you have identified the cause of your stress.

Discovering the relationship between lifestyle and stress

American cardiologists, Meyer Friedman and Ray Rosenman, were the first to propose that the way you behave is the most important predictor of whether you will develop heart disease (a disease to which stress is a major contributory factor). They discovered that many people who suffer from heart disease have similar behavior patterns, as a result of their mix of personality, lifestyle, and attitude.

Their model of type A and type B behavior has been widely used to help understand the link between behavior and stress. Type A and B behavior is now well established in both medical and business literature.

The two types of people

Type A behavior is characterized by a driving sense of urgency. Often type A people come across as aggressive, competitive, and ambitious.

Type B behavior is characterized by a much more relaxed attitude toward life. Type B people tend to be slower moving, more patient, generally easy going, and relaxed. Rosenman and Friedman found that 50 percent of the people they studied fell into the type A category, 40 percent into type B, and 10 percent somewhere between the two. This statistic was the same for both sexes.

Which type is more successful?

The Rosenman and Friedman study showed that more people with jobs at the very top of large companies were type B – a fact that has since been corroborated by other research findings. Maybe you need type A behavior in order to climb up the corporate ladder; but, once you are there, you can relax more, and feel more at ease with yourself.

Having established the type A and B behavior patterns, Rosenman and Friedman then took a sample of more than 3,000 people. They selected an even split between type As and Bs and followed them up over the next ten years. At the end of this period, they discovered that the type A people had suffered more than three times as many heart attacks as the type B people. Certain lifestyles encourage particular behavior patterns. Many people in business feel that they have to behave like a type A person to succeed.

Types of organizations

This method of classification can be extended to companies and organizations. The culture, management style, and method of operating within an organization will reflect the two different behavior patterns. In the 1980s and early 1990s, the trend in many corporate cultures was towards a more type A management style.

It can be stressful working for an organization where the culture does not match your own personality type. A type B person will find it difficult to cope in a driven and aggressive environment, but a type A person may find a relaxed workplace frustrating.

A Day In The Life Of Roger "Type A"

Many research studies reveal that business life makes many demands on our health. These two case studies will help you to build a picture of type A and B people. As you read them, think of yourself and people around you; and see if you recognize any of the behavior patterns.

Leaving home

Roger is up and out of the house in 15 or 20 minutes, depending on whether he can find an ironed shirt. Breakfast is snatched from the toaster on his way out. He hates hanging around when he knows there is work to be done.

Arriving at work

Because his secretary is not in, Roger makes coffee and goes through the unsorted mail. Anything that is for him he opens, reads, and leaves in the in-tray for further action. He does the really quick and easy things immediately, because he must move on. It is relatively quiet in the office, so he does about half an hour of uninterrupted work on the presentation he has to give at 10:30 a.m. Unfortunately, just as he is about to do a quick rehearsal, the telephone rings; and he is distracted. In fact, this phone call marks the start of the series of interruptions. Easy questions get quick answers, but more difficult ones get put off with promises of further investigation and action. Roger prides himself on never having to say no. He does recognize that, because his attention tends to switch rapidly between numerous areas, his concentration level remains relatively low.

In the meeting

Roger has to run to make his 10:30 a.m. meeting and is glad to see that one or two people are later than he is. His presentation goes well, though it would have been nice to have slides. But, as always, his confidence and energy win the day. Although everyone else was most impressed, Roger secretly worries that one of these days he will fail to snatch success from the jaws of disaster.

Lunchtime

Roger rarely finds time to get out for a break at lunch, and today is no exception. His lunch is a sandwich at his desk.

In the office he gets a phone call from his boss. She reminds him of a report she delegated to him and requests an update by 2:00 p.m. He had completely forgotten about it and works through lunch in order to cover his embarrassment. Roger manages to bluff his way through the meeting with a promise of more work on the report over the weekend.

When he returns to his office his in-tray is so full that even he realizes that he is not going to be able to get through all his work.

Managing the team

Roger decides to delegate the more urgent work to his team. He feels quite happy doing this because people are always saying that he should delegate more work. But two of the team members are a little upset because they have booked a squash court for 5:30 p.m. and will now have to cancel. The potential mutiny is quickly crushed with a reminder of the unemployment figures and the fact that he, himself, rarely gets away from the office before 7p.m. Roger takes no nonsense from his team!

The rest of the afternoon flies by in a whirlwind of activity, and it is only after everyone has gone home that Roger again manages to get on with some uninterrupted work. Unfortunately, he is unable to make progress on the most important project in his in-box. It requires some information from a client, but Roger missed them when he phoned at 5:45 p.m. Nevertheless, there are many other things in his in-box to keep him busy until 7:30 p.m.

Going home

Suddenly, Roger realizes that today is his wedding anniversary, and he's late. At that precise moment, the phone rings. Luckily for Roger, it is his wife, telling him that she will be late because she has to remain at the office to resolve a crisis. Once again Roger's luck has held!

KEY EVENTS IN THE DAY

Leaving home
- Rushing out of the house
- No planning
- No proper breakfast

Arriving at work
- Dives straight in
- Makes quick decisons
- Easily distracted
- Takes on too many tasks

The meeting
- Last-minute preparation
- Lots of confidence
- Thinks on his feet

Lunchtime
- No lunch break

Managing his team
- Last minute delegation
- Makes unfair demands
- Doesn't listen

Going home
- Works late
- No time for his family

A Day In The Life Of Harry "Type B"

Harry starts the day at a leisurely pace. He helps his wife get the children up and takes time to sit down for breakfast with his family. Harry makes it a priority to enjoy life.

Leaving home

Harry likes to allow plenty of time to get to the office. He has invested in a good car radio and sees the slow drive to work as time well spent. He uses it to keep up to date on current affairs by listening to the news or relaxing with music.

Arriving at work

Upon arrival at his office, Harry spends some time chatting to his secretary and other members of his team under the guise of a daily briefing. He is happy giving directions, but he rarely makes decisions without a lot of deliberation. The meeting takes longer than necessary and ends without clear action points.

Once Harry gets into his office he is difficult to dislodge. His powers of concentration are impressive and his eye for detail sometimes borders on the fanatical. It has become a standing joke that he rarely approves any work until it has been drafted five times.

Harry has to make a presentation to the Board at 10:30 a.m., and he is not confident. He has set aside an hour to go through his material and make final revisions. He still is not happy with the script and makes one or two late changes. He goes down to the meeting room about 15 minutes early to run through his material one final time.

In the meeting

Harry's slot is just after his colleague Roger, whose presentations always make Harry feel thoroughly inadequate. He has often seen Roger present without visual aids or notes, Harry is tempted to try the same. Fortunately he resists.

Everyone seems impressed, but he would have liked them to be more enthusiastic. He wonders whether they failed to grasp the finer points.

Lunchtime

Harry goes out for lunch with a client. He enjoys doing business over lunch and feels it is important to know his clients. He believes they hire him because they like him.

The afternoon

On returning to the office Harry finds a note from his boss reminding him that he has been asked for estimates of next year's expenses by 3:00 p.m. Harry has already worked out some preliminary figures, but he is unsure how to present them and is worried about all the variables that could affect them. He goes to see his boss to talk them through. His boss is busy, and Harry's figures are dismissed as far too complicated.

Harry passes two of Roger's team members in the hall. They are upset and, because Harry is a good listener, they pour out their grievances to him. He sympathizes – without being disloyal to Roger. How anyone can be so hard on their staff he cannot imagine!

When Harry gets back to his office he finds a document he delegated to a member of his team back in his in-box. He feels that, as usual, he does not seem to have explained what he wanted well enough and rewrites it. By the time he finishes he has missed the outgoing mail and has to send it by courier.

Going home

Harry's in-box is full of small bits and pieces that have been collecting throughout the day – a number of trivial issues that require fast decisions. However, it is 5:30 p.m., so Harry tidies his desk and leaves. He likes to be home before the children are in bed.

Harry reflects that he is unlikely to get to the top of the corporate ladder, but he wonders what good this type of success is if you are too busy to enjoy it?

KEY EVENTS IN THE DAY

Leaving home
- Relaxed
- Spends time with his family
- Eats a proper breakfast

Arriving at work
- Plans his day
- Slow decision maker
- Able to concentrate
- Obsessed with detail

The meeting
- Thorough preparation
- Lacks confidence
- Doesn't always make an impact

Lunchtime
- Eats a proper lunch
- Makes time for clients

Managing his team
- Approachable
- Listens well
- Lacks clarity
- Obsessed with quality

Going home
- Leaves on time
- Spends time with his family
- Feels happy with himself

Work Pattern Self-Assessment

We can all probably recognize one or two people among our friends and colleagues who are extreme examples of a type A or B personality. The majority of people have a core personality type, to which we will usually return even if we manage to temporarily override our natural tendencies in particular situations. This core personality type is usually a mixture of type A and B behavior. Perhaps you exhibit different types of behavior depending upon the situation? It is not unusual, for example, to adopt type A characteristics at work, but type B behavior at home. Perhaps the kind of work you do requires type A behavior, even though you are mainly a type B personality, or maybe the corporate culture in your organization demands that you behave in a way that doesn't necessarily feel natural to you. This can be stressful. It can also be difficult for people of extreme personality types to work closely together, unless each makes the effort to understand the other. However, these differences can produce an excellent working partnership.

Statement A	Score					Statement B
My definition of success is the achievement of measurable goals.	1	2	3	4	5	Success depends on a number of factors, few of which are measurable.
When I put myself under pressure, I find myself jumping between a number of pieces of work.	1	2	3	4	5	Even when time is tight, I like to finish one piece of work completely before moving on.
I feel most comfortable with numerically measurable success criteria.	1	2	3	4	5	The important things in life are too complex to measure numerically.
The major factors in my success are my confidence and energy.	1	2	3	4	5	My major contribution is my eye for detail.
The future is in my hands. It is up to me to work hard and make the most of it.	1	2	3	4	5	By always striving for the future I might miss the pleasures of the present.

How Did You Score?

SCORING METHOD

This questionnaire will help to identify your character type and develop a more effective work pattern. Read each pair of statements and decide which is most like you. If statement A or B sums you up, circle 1 or 5. If you are somewhere in between, circle an appropriate number. Answer quickly and avoid too many 3s.

How did you score?

10-14	strong type A
15-24	tends towards type A
25-34	mixed type behavior
35-44	tendency towards type B
45-50	strong type B

Statement A	Score	Statement B
I like to be No. 1 and naturally compete with others for that spot.	1 2 3 4 5	I do not need to be No.1 to prove my worth, therefore I am rarely competitive.
If people do not perform as I wish, I am quick to confront them.	1 2 3 4 5	There is usually a good reason when people fail to perform, so rather than get angry I try to find out what that reason is.
When stating their case, people should be brief and say only what is relevant. If they don't, I tend to interrupt.	1 2 3 4 5	I am a good listener and hardly ever get impatient or interrupt.
I hate sitting around doing nothing and would far rather be busy.	1 2 3 4 5	I know that by driving harder I could achieve more, but am not prepared to give up my free time in order to do so.
It takes an imminent deadline to get me really working.	1 2 3 4 5	If you want me to produce really good work, don't pressure me with a deadline.

Your Job and Stress

Studies have shown certain occupations to be more stressful than others, and certain aspects within each occupation to cause stress. Most people know someone who has changed jobs because he or she found the current one too stressful. Take a look at your job, and see if any aspects of it are a source of stress for you.

Structure of the organization

How comfortable are you in the organization for which you work? Does it have a culture that helps you perform effectively? Is the organization too large, making you believe that you have no influence? Is it too small, restricting your opportunities to progress? Bureaucracy can be frustrating and inhibiting, but some people prefer rules and regulations to a looser environment.

Relationships at work

How well do you get on with your boss, your team and clients? A lot of your time may be spent with people at work. If relationships there are tense, it can be very draining and stressful. Are there particular people you find it hard to get along with?

Career development

Your job should give you the opportunity for the career progress you want. Job security may be the most important factor for some people, while others are more ambitious. If you are not going the way you would like to go, this can be a source of stress.

Clarity of job role

If there is a lack of clarity about your role in your job, this can lead to all kinds of problems with relationships with colleagues, confusion, time management and more. Be sure that you know exactly what is expected of you.

Other factors

Many factors can contribute to stress at work. Poor working conditions, noise, physical danger, an office move, or simply having too much to do can all be difficult to cope with. Levels of pay are also a common cause of stress.

ASK YOURSELF:
- Is work the largest part of my life?
- Am I happy with this?
- Am I making time for all the other things I want out of life?
- Does work allow me to meet my needs?
- Do I want a different balance between work and non-work?
- In an ideal world, what would the balance of my life look like?
- What changes do I need to make?
- What am I going to do to make the changes?
- Once the changes have been made, what will be different?

Taking stock

For many people, work is a major part of
life. Unhappiness in any aspect of your
work life may lead to stress and have a
trickle-down effect on other aspects of
your life – relationships and health, for
example. Review your work regularly to
assess whether you are happy in your job.
There just aren't enough hours in the
day, days in a year, years in a lifetime!
Don't waste them in a job that causes
you stress.

Managing your career

You must manage your career to ensure
that you get what you want out of life.
Organizations are increasingly adopting
more flattened management structures,
which offer fewer opportunities for the
more traditional career paths.

Working patterns generally are
changing and with them the opportunity
to create the type of job that suits you is
growing. Many of the traditional
assumptions about careers are changing,
as well.

Changing jobs

Changing jobs is never easy, particularly
in a competitive and insecure job
market. But if your job is making you
unhappy and causing stress, you should
seriously consider making changes.

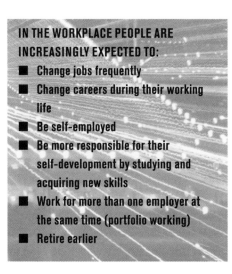

**IN THE WORKPLACE PEOPLE ARE
INCREASINGLY EXPECTED TO:**
- Change jobs frequently
- Change careers during their working
  life
- Be self-employed
- Be more responsible for their
  self-development by studying and
  acquiring new skills
- Work for more than one employer at
  the same time (portfolio working)
- Retire earlier

Think of your life as a
clock. Time is ticking by –
you'll never have it again.
How much time are you
giving to the different
aspects of your life?

Take a look at your objectives in life
and what you want to achieve. What is
important to you – both inside and
outside of work?

If you like your current employer but
not the job, it may not be necessary to
change companies. Instead, you could
seek ways of changing or developing
your role within your present
organization. An internal transfer could
be the answer to your problems. Many
organizations post the job openings
internally. Make sure you keep your eye
out for other jobs that open up within
the company.

You may also consider retraining to
acquire the necessary new skills and
qualifications once you have decided on
the new job you are seeking.

Your Job And Stress

Take on additional responsibilities if you feel that you are not being fully utilized. Volunteer for projects and new responsibilities, and ask to be included in areas that will help to develop your skills and raise your profile.

If you are not happy where you are, the answer may be a move to a different branch or office. This type of move can have the advantage of giving you a chance to make a fresh start, while retaining the familiarity of working in an organization you know.

If you feel stuck in a rut, it may be possible to seek opportunities to travel more with your present employer. Perhaps you could increase visits to clients, suppliers, or other branches.

Promotion

Promotion can make or break you! In the short term it can cause an increase in demands and pressure. It is important to manage this change effectively. Make sure you set clear goals and objectives in your new position to avoid feelings of confusion or disappointment.

It is up to you to take the initiative to ensure that you have a good transition. Make sure that you have plenty of opportunity for support from your predecessor and, if appropriate, from the previous post-holder. Also, arrange for a well-planned and thorough transfer of responsibilities to the person taking over your previous position. You do not want to find yourself "straddling" the two jobs for any longer than is necessary. It is essential to let go of your previous responsibilities so that you can concentrate on new ones. If you will need new skills, organize any training you think will be necessary for both the long- and short-term.

Because promotion will, initially, place additional demands on you, it is important to manage all other aspects of your life. Once you become familiar with your new job, you can resume the former pace of all your other activities.

Demotion

The loss of status caused by demotion is likely to be very stressful. It can affect relationships and have difficult financial consequences. It is essential that you take steps to minimize your stress at such a trying time.

Career ceilings

Frustration about not being promoted or having no promotion prospects is another source of stress. There are many other reasons why people do not manage to progress in their careers. Perhaps you are simply in the wrong job, or working for the wrong organization.

As many organizations flatten their managerial structure, the conventional career path is available to fewer people. The observation that you have gone as far as you can go in your organization and you are only 40 is an increasingly common one.

Take steps to manage your stress when you come up against a career ceiling or suffer a demotion.

Don't bottle up your emotions. Talk about your feelings with family and managers. The old cliché is true: a problem shared is often a problem halved. Develop new coping strategies and social networks to help yourself during this time. Be kind to yourself. Treats, at a time like this, can lighten a heavy burden.

Try to think positively about the options available. Set yourself clear goals and action plans; work on the things that you are able to change; and leave the ones you can't change. Develop the skills you need to put yourself in a good position when new opportunities present themselves.

MOST STRESSFUL JOBS

prison guard
police officer
social worker
teacher
ambulance driver
nurse
doctor
fire fighter
dentist
miner
soldier
construction worker
actor
journalist

LEAST STRESSFUL JOBS

astronomer
beauty operator
conservationist
horticulturalist
librarian
museum worker
hairdresser
podiatrist
sports/recreation administrator
optician
osteopath
church worker

Work-Stress Questionnaire

Pressure from your work commitments is one of the most common causes of stress. You spend a great deal of your time at work; and, if you feel anxious, unable to cope or dissatisfied, this will add to your stress.

Think objectively about your job and the parts of it you find difficult. Are there certain tasks or responsibilities that make you anxious?

By completing the questionnaire you will be able to identify these general areas more easily and examine the overall impact of stress on your job. This is the first step in deciding how you can change the situation you are faced with. If you are generally dissatisfied with your job, the questions below should help you prioritize the aspects you need to work on.

Answer the questions as honestly as you can. Going through the table quite quickly, without agonizing over the answers, will help you.

	Question	Score		Question	Score
1	How often do you feel you have too little authority to carry out your responsibilities?		6	How often do you feel that you are not fully qualified to handle your job?	
2	How often do you feel you are unclear about the scope and responsibilities of your job?		7	How often do you not know what your superior thinks of you or how he or she evaluates your performance?	
3	How often are you unaware that opportunities for advancement and promotion exist for you?		8	How often do you find yourself unable to get the information you need to perform your job?	
4	How often do you feel that you have too heavy a workload, one that you could not possibly finish during an ordinary work day?		9	How often do you worry about making decisions that affect the lives of people you know?	
5	How often do you feel that you will not be able to satisfy the conflicting demands of various people around you?		10	How often do you feel that you may not be liked and accepted by people at work?	

Scoring Method

Write the score which best matches your behaviour according to the following scheme:

1 = never

2 = seldom

3 = sometimes

4 = often

5 = nearly all the time

	Question	Score
11	How often do you feel unable to influence your immediate supervisor's decisions and actions that affect you?	
12	How often do you not know just what the people you work with expect of you?	
13	How often do you think the amount of work you have to do may interfere with how well it is done?	
14	How often do you feel that you have to do things on the job that are against your better judgement?	
15	How often do you feel your job interferes with your family life?	

What Your Score Means

15–30

A low score indicates that you are experiencing little pressure at work and generally feel in control.

31–45

This range indicates a good level of control most of the time. Situations cause stress occasionally.

46–60

This range indicates that you often feel under pressure and out of control. At this level it is quite likely you will suffer some form of stress.

61–75

This range indicates a high level of pressure and feelings of being out of control. You will almost certainly be suffering from stress.

Managing Your Reactions

You might take the advice of your doctor or friends to rest more, take a holiday, eat better food, meditate, jog, or play squash. Such approaches certainly help, but they do not get to the root of the problem. Stress is more than a simple cause–effect reaction. The inner dimension of this process – your expectations, beliefs, perceptions, and needs – is also a key factor in the equation. This opens up another way of handling stress.

For example, in a traffic jam, rather than seeing the situation as a threat and wishing it would go away, you could ask yourself, "What is the opportunity here? What is the best use of my time?" You could then trigger a different set of reactions, such as listening to a new piece of music you haven't had time to enjoy before or mentally preparing for the meeting ahead. You would still arrive at work late but in a considerably less stressed state.

If you see stress as a purely negative thing and a barrier to functioning, you will tend to manage only its outer manifestations, its causes, and its effects. If, however, you see it as an opportunity to learn more about yourself and what is really important to you, it can become another window into yourself. Stress can be a signal that there is still more to learn about your inner world.

	Statement	Score		Statement	Score
1	I am generally more nervous than other people.		6	I notice my heart pounding and shortness of breath.	
2	I regularly suffer from headaches.		7	I have stomach troubles.	
3	I work under a great deal of pressure.		8	I have had periods when I have lost sleep because of my worries.	
4	I worry about money and business.		9	I frequently find myself worried or upset by things.	
5	I sweat very easily even on cool days.		10	I tire quickly.	

Scoring Method

Some indications of stress are listed in the table.
To establish your general level give your response to the statements as honestly as you can.

Use the following scale:

1 = Strongly disagree

2 = Disagree

3 = Not sure

4 = Agree

5 = Strongly agree

What Your Score Means

15–30

A low score means that you are a relaxed person and not likely to be suffering from stress.

31–45

This range indicates a good level of control most of the time. Some situations cause stress occasionally. Look again at the questions where you scored the highest.

46–60

This range means you suffer from stress and are likely to be experiencing some stress-related illnesses.

61–75

This range indicates a high level of stress. You will very likely suffer from some stress-related illness.

	Statement	Score
11	I wish I could be as happy as other people seem to be.	
12	I feel that difficulties are piling up so high that I cannot overcome them.	
13	I have at times worried about something that did not really matter.	
14	Sometimes I feel useless.	
15	I am inclined to react badly.	

Identify Sources of Stress

Identify the major causes of stress in your life at this time. This will be easier if you think of the various aspects of your life. The self-imposed stressors are mainly the ones you create in your mind – your perceptions about yourself and your abilities.

Current stressors in my life

From your reading and thinking so far, pick two or three key stressors from each aspect of your life. Try and identify the underlying causes of the stress. This will help you understand why it causes you stress and develop a plan of action to tackle it. This might be quite difficult and painful, but is crucial if you wish to move on in your life.

Prioritize your stress

Divide the stressors into three categories. This will help you decide how best to manage them. Beware of putting too many entries in the "must live with" section. You may have to live with an event, such as the death of a loved one or the loss of a job, but you don't have to live with a negative self-image or a difficult work relationship.

Personal signs and symptoms

What are your trigger points, both mental and physical, when you are under stress? Work on the causes as well as tackling the symptoms.

My current coping strategies

What do you do now when you are suffering from stress or feeling anxious? We all develop some strategies to use when faced with a stressful situation – go for a walk, count to ten, talk with your friends, or play a game of golf. These are all positive reactions and ones you should recognize and develop.

Changing our lives

This exercise is the first stage of developing a plan to help reduce your levels of stress and counteract anxiety. Often, it is not until we are faced with the cold facts that we take action.

We can go through many years of suffering before we realize the impact it is having on us and on our lives. Stress can be doing its damage without our even noticing it. For example, years of working late and coming home after the children have gone to bed may have become a part of life, but is it what you really want? Are you prepared for the effect it may have in the future? It may not be until the children have grown up and left home that you realize what you have missed out on and the damage to your relationships because of working late for so many years.

Use this exercise to really help you change your life. It is up to you to take responsibility and make the changes. Nobody else will do it for you.

CURRENT STRESSORS IN MY LIFE

Home

_____

_____

_____

Work

_____

_____

_____

Self

_____

_____

_____

_____

PERSONAL SIGNS AND SYMPTOMS

Physical

_____

_____

_____

Mental

_____

_____

_____

_____

SUMMARY

Stresses I must live with

_____

_____

_____

Ones on which I can have a partial impact

_____

_____

_____

Ones over which I have complete control

_____

_____

_____

MY CURRENT COPING STRATEGIES ARE:

_____

_____

_____

_____

_____

_____

DO YOU RECOGNIZE ANY OF THESE SOURCES OF STRESS?

- Too much work to do
- Taking work home
- Unproductive meetings
- Time wasting
- Interruptions
- Work never completed
- Poor communications
- Poor working conditions
- No time to relax
- Little physical exercise
- No hobbies or pastimes
- Rarely visiting friends or relatives
- Never time to sit and read the papers
- Rarely going to the movies or theater
- Never doing anything different

Moving Forward

The next section of the book moves on from understanding stress to taking action. You should now have a better understanding of what stress is and what it is not.

Defining stress

Stress may result from activities we choose to do or from things that are imposed on us. A great deal of stress comes from what happens in our head – our thought processes. Managing stress is about balancing the demands placed on you and your ability to cope.

Controlling stress

You have assessed where stress comes from in your life. The events that cause it at work, at home, and in your personal life are, to some degree at least, within your own control. When managing stress, it is sensible to work on those issues over which we do have control and learn to live with those we don't.

Lifestyle and stress

The way you live your life will also have an impact on how well you cope with pressure and how much you suffer from stress. This includes home, work, your general health, and personal relationships. If your lifestyle is particularly stress inducing, think about how you can change it for the better.

A framework for action

You now need to move and make practical changes to your life to help reduce stress. Making changes will involve making choices. Some choices will be more difficult than others. Having examined the options, you may decide to do nothing. Deciding not to make the choice is, in itself, a choice. Feeling trapped is very stressful. Knowing there is a way out, whether you take it or not, can be stress relieving in itself.

The rest of the book focuses on the practical action you can take to tackle stress. You will be most successful if you use a four-pronged attack to combat each of your stressors (right).

Attack the cause Find out the root cause of a stressful situation. Once you understand the real cause you can take action. By changing the situation you can remove the stress.

Developing coping strategies Are you equipping yourself with all the skills you need to be able to cope with the demands being placed on you? This may require developing specific skills, such as writing reports, giving presentations, or chairing meetings. Alternatively, it may be broader behavioral skills you need, such as improving your ability to be assertive or communicate.

Working on your mind By recognizing the stress you place on yourself with your own thoughts, you can change the way you think and therefore reduce stress. You need to analyze the damage that negative thoughts are doing and "reprogram" your mind.

Balance your lifestyle If you want your body to function properly and be able to cope with pressure, you must look after it. This means managing the environment you live in, the food you eat, and the way you relax. You are in control of these aspects of your life.

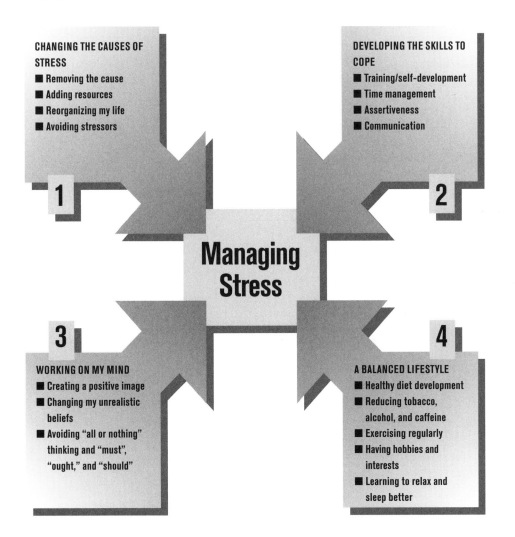

CHANGING THE CAUSES OF STRESS
- Removing the cause
- Adding resources
- Reorganizing my life
- Avoiding stressors

1

DEVELOPING THE SKILLS TO COPE
- Training/self-development
- Time management
- Assertiveness
- Communication

2

Managing Stress

3

WORKING ON MY MIND
- Creating a positive image
- Changing my unrealistic beliefs
- Avoiding "all or nothing" thinking and "must", "ought," and "should"

4

A BALANCED LIFESTYLE
- Healthy diet development
- Reducing tobacco, alcohol, and caffeine
- Exercising regularly
- Having hobbies and interests
- Learning to relax and sleep better

3

Avoid stressors
Add resources
Organize
Modify behavior

Will changing my life reduce stress?

How can I attack the causes of stress?

Can I modify my behavior?

Attack the Causes of Stress

Stress is not just something you have to live with. In most cases, it can be reduced by taking direct action to remove the causes of stress from your life.

Adding resources

Lighten the load by adding resources. This may mean equipment or materials, such as a fax machine or some new software. Help from other people can be a valuable resource. Perhaps family or friends could help look after your children, or someone who is being under utilized in their job may be able to take on some of your workload.

It may not always be possible to add resources, but unless you try you won't find out. Consider this case:

An office worker estimated that she spent at least an hour each day going from her office to the mail room to collect faxes. She realized that getting a fax machine in her office would save her valuable time, but she believed her boss would never agree to it. When she was finally persuaded to ask, her boss immediately said yes. In fact, there was a spare fax machine in another office that wasn't being used.

Could you organize for less stress?

Reorganizing your home or work environment can reduce your stress levels. Could you improve your seating or the position of your desk at work? Would sharing the household tasks among all members of the family or arranging to have groceries delivered lighten your load?

Open-plan offices can be particularly distracting, especially when work requires a great deal of concentration. Finding a quiet place can mean that a report that normally takes several days to write could be completed more quickly. The quality would also be improved if you are not constantly interrupted.

Perhaps you could arrange to do particularly complex tasks at home. Not only will you save travel time, you will probably have fewer interruptions. As an alternative, try to book a meeting room or use a vacant office.

Avoiding particular stressors

Avoidance, or flight, may be the best way to escape the intolerable pressures of an unsatisfactory job, a poor relationship, or bad living conditions. You may need to avoid certain people in your life who cause you stress. Take stock of your current relationships with family, friends, and colleagues.

Consider the following example of taking action to avoid stressors in one's life. A product manager in a company found it difficult to deal with a supplier. Their personalities clashed, and as a consequence, the business suffered.

Meetings would always turn into arguments. The product manager would dread the supplier's telephone calls and get angry with himself. Many evenings were spoiled by a meeting during the day or the thought of one tomorrow.

The product manager worked as part of a team and, after discussion, the team reorganized. The product manager took on other tasks, while a colleague took over the relationship with that supplier. With the new working relationship, business improved. Most importantly, this major source of stress was removed from the product manager's life.

You may need to make important changes to your life. Your own behavior pattern may be an underlying source of anxiety. Could you change the excesses of type A or type B behavior? Could you move from an unsatisfactory job or area or arrange to work flextime to avoid rush-hour traffic?

Subtracting the causes of stress

By subtracting the sources of stress, we remove the effects. It is easy to become involved in a repetitive pattern of behavior. It is more difficult to take a fresh look at your life and remove them.

By cutting down the time spent in meetings you can probably remove a major source of stress at work. Meetings can be stressful simply because they take up precious time or put demands on you to perform. Go through your daily planner for the past three months, and critically examine the meetings you have attended. Ask yourself whether you really needed to go. Could you have delegated attending? Could you have been excused and simply received the minutes instead?

Long commutes are also a common source of stress. Consider the following case: A city worker commuted to the city center every day which involved leaving home every morning at 6:15 a.m. and returning home after 8:00 p.m. The trip at each end of the day took an hour and a half. This started to take its toll on his health, producing a variety of stress symptoms. The dream of a house in the country was not worth the stress, so he moved into the city. It was a decision he never regretted.

There is rarely a simple answer to any complex problem. Extreme forms of coping behavior, such as moving, changing job, or leaving a partner can create new problems. Each individual has to decide whether, on balance, it is worth substituting one set of problems for another.

AVOIDING OR ATTACKING STRESS?

Avoiding the source of stress does not remove it completely, it is really a form of first aid. Avoidance can see you through the short term, but it is rarely a long-term solution. You may have to tackle the underlying causes of stress to bring lasting relief. For example, if you find making presentations stressful, you probably can get out of doing them. However, it will probably be more worthwhile in the long run to think about what it is about making presentations that makes you anxious and to tackle these underlying causes.

Modify Type A Behavior

If type A behavior is a key cause of stress the question you must ask is, "Can type A behavior be modified or altered?" The answer is Yes! By changing only a few aspects of type A behavior, not only can you reduce your stress levels, you can also become more effective at work.

Work control

Type A people usually take on lots of work without thinking of time, budget, or staffing. Once you have brought some order to your life, review regularly. Reduce an impossible work schedule by utilizing your planner and keeping it up to date, keeping meetings short, and taking lunch breaks. Learn to say "no" without feeling guilty. Before committing to something, take a moment to think about the consequences.

Delegation

Type A people often leave delegation to the last minute, believing that they can do the job quicker and better themselves. When delegating work, plan early, think through the task first, fully brief the person, and review his or her progress regularly without hovering.

Learn to listen

You have two ears and one mouth. Try to teach yourself to use them in these proportions: listen rather than talk.

Develop your active listening skills and make an effort to be open and receptive. Don't fold your arms when you are listening (this is a defensive posture) and, if seated, lean slightly forward to convey your interest.

Try to face the person you are listening to and make good eye contact. Respond occasionally, nodding your head or repeating words.

In meetings, it may help to keep a few notes when people are talking.

Planning

"All my work is high priority" is a classic type A comment. If you don't prioritize you will end up "butterflying" through the day, starting many things but finishing only a few. If you keep a "to do" list, it is important to rank order the various tasks on it; otherwise you will tend to focus on the ones you enjoy or take less time. This means that you will leave the real high-priority tasks until the end.

Relaxing

Some type A people think they spend lots of time relaxing, but their hobbies can be stressful in themselves. One example is competitive squash. Make time to relax and don't feel guilty about it. Walking, massage, and meditation are all stress relievers and are generally not engaged in by type A people.

WORK CONTROL

■ Keep meetings short.
■ Keep your work daily planner up to date.
■ Restrict your work load.
■ Don't say yes without thinking about the implications for yourself and the team.
■ Learn to say no without guilt.
■ Do not accept unrealistic deadlines.

DELEGATION

■ Assess your workload and pinpoint tasks that can be delegated.
■ Give other people the opportunity to take on new responsibilities.
■ Delegate in plenty of time.
■ Provide a thorough set of instructions.
■ Resist the temptation to interfere.
■ Plan review dates, and stick to them.

PLANNING

■ Make a "to do" list each day.
■ Pay attention to details.
■ Prioritize your day's workload.
■ Try to be realistic about timelines.
■ Resist the temptation to do easy tasks or those you enjoy first.
■ Break down large tasks into small, manageable, pieces and plan each one.

RELAXING

■ Make time for relaxation a priority.
■ Make sure that your mind and body are given a chance to switch off and regenerate.
■ Plan a regular quiet time into your daily work program.
■ Remember that effective relaxation will make you more productive at work.
■ Learn to sit back and let others take control sometimes.

Modify Type B Behavior

Some aspects of type B behavior may also lead to stress, and type B personalities can take steps in key areas to reduce stress.

Setting goals

Type B personalities are thorough and professional but can drift through life. This can cause stress when they don't achieve what they want to. Set clear goals and try to make sure you know where you are going so that your talent and energy are not wasted. At the start of the day set goals for that day. Make sure the goals are specific, measurable, achievable, realistic, and time-based. Having set the goal, give yourself a start time, and review progress regularly.

Delegation

This can also be a problem. Type B personalities are reluctant to let go because they don't trust other people. Often when they delegate, the briefing is vague; and the results are not what they wanted. Be clear in the briefing. Don't overbrief and get bogged down in too much detail. Let the person use his or her skills and creativity.

Don't feel guilty when delegating. If you hang on to everything yourself, your team will become demotivated.

When the task is completed don't be too "picky." It may not be exactly as you would have done it; it may be better!

People management

Type Bs need to be more assertive when dealing with difficult people or difficult situations. Don't feel guilty about saying "no," making difficult decisions, or reprimanding people if it is part of your job. Not all dealings with people are easy. Deal with problems as they arise. Don't sit on them in the hope that they will go away. The longer they are left alone the worse they will get.

Be direct with the other person, giving him or her a clear message. Don't apologize for taking a firm line; it only weakens your case and could lead to pointless discussion. Don't feel nervous or guilty when you discipline. You have a duty to your staff to provide strong, fair management; and it achieves results.

Quality

Learn when enough is enough. It is not always necessary to give the best possible answer to a question. Sometimes just a good answer will do!

Stick to the brief question or issue. Don't go off on a tangent. Assess what is needed at the outset and stick to it. Resist the temptation to add too many details or "extras." Get the basics right first.

Make sure you have really understood what is required of you.

Bring tasks to an end. When writing a report, for example, avoid going back, rewriting, and adding more.

SETTING CLEAR GOALS

■ Set long-term goals for yourself regularly.

■ Give yourself a timetable, and stick to it.

■ Review your progress.

■ Goals must be clear and achievable.

■ Set daily goals.

■ Do not waste your time and energy on tasks that are irrelevant to your goals.

DELEGATION

■ Don't try to do everything yourself.

■ Avoid over-long and complicated directions.

■ Resist the temptation to interfere.

■ Allow the person doing the job to use his or her own initiative and ideas.

■ Do not be too fussy about the final result, or expect it to match exactly how you would have done it.

PEOPLE MANAGEMENT

■ Do not give credit or praise unless it is deserved.

■ Do not avoid dealing with problems.

■ Do not apologize when taking a firm line.

■ Fair management is a duty, so do not feel guilty if you have to use discipline.

■ Be direct and clear when dealing with problem areas or staff.

QUALITY

■ Make sure you know what is required of you.

■ Ask questions to make sure you understand the directions.

■ Follow to the directions.

■ Do not be tempted to add lots of extras at the expense of the basics.

■ Bring the task to an end.

Goal setting is not about vague ideas and "nice to" thoughts. It is about hard thinking and ideas. Goals should be SMART goals.

S specific

M measurable

A achievable

R realistic

T time-based

Write your goals down. It is the first step to making them happen.

4

Assertiveness
Communication
Relaxation
Massage

Can I cope better with stress?

Can I manage my time better?

How can I be more assertive?

Develop Skills to Cope at Work

Think about situations you find stressful, and try to develop some skills to manage them. This may involve attending a course (through work or privately), reading a self-development book, or following a guided-learning program on video or computer. If the main cause of your stress is work-related, ask a colleague to help you overcome the problems. Here are some suggestions for how to cope with common situations at work.

Create a productive environment

A chaotic desk or workspace can waste a lot of time, make you less efficient, and convey a poor impression to others.

Desk equipment If you know you are easily distracted by executive toys, the phone, your computer terminal or an in-box, move them out of your reach or sight.

Desk orientation You don't always have a choice; but, if possible, ensure that your desk is not facing a door, photocopier, fax machine, or any other piece of frequently used equipment. This will help to reduce the distractions and improve your work rate.

Organize your work

Small changes in working practices can dramatically increase your efficiency and are simple to implement.

Paperwork The more paperwork you have on your desk, the more inefficient you are likely to be. You will waste time searching for information. Empty your in-box two or three times a day. Do not deal with every individual piece of work as it comes in because you will be distracted. As a result, numerous things will be partly done, and few will be actually completed.

Pitch-it day Set a regular time for a general tidying up and throwing out session. For example, designate the last day of the month or the end of an accounting period to sort through things and throw out what you do not need.

Bring-forward system Rather than keeping paper on your desk for periods of time, develop a bring-forward system. When a piece of paper comes in, decide when you are going to deal with it. If you are not going to deal with it immediately, file it and put a note in your planner on the day you intend to work on it. When you come into the office each day, check in your planner, get out the papers, and work on them. Some people use accordian files, divided by day of the week, to organize their work.

Filing "A little and often" should be your motto. Don't let filing build up, or it will become a chore.

Control interruptions

A constant stream of interruptions can put you under an enormous amount of pressure. Open-plan offices encourage interruptions. The effect of having so many people in one room is that distractions from other people and irrelevant interruptions are commonplace. As well as causing stress, interruptions reduce productivity. However, you can take control and reduce the impact of interruptions on your working day.

It is important to take a balanced view of the importance of your work in relation to the needs of other people. Too little emphasis on your own work will lead to disruption.

Position yourself to avoid interruptions. Try and situate your desk away from obvious "people collection" points, such as photocopiers and fax machines, so that you are less likely to get caught up in other people's breaks. Having spare chairs around your desk is an invitation to anyone who wants to sit down for a chat. If you cannot avoid having the chair, try and keep books and papers on it when you want to be left alone to work.

Find a quiet space to get on with work that requires deep concentration. You may need to find a spare office or meeting room when you want some uninterrupted time.

Limit the damage Encourage someone who is interrupting you to get to the point. You can use body language to control interruptions. Stand up as soon as somebody comes to your desk. The reason is more likely to be brief, and you will feel more assertive in dealing with the situation. Alternatively, perch on your desk. This can give a nonaggressive signal that your time is precious and you intend this to be very quick.

Delay the interruption If the interruption is less important than your work, delay dealing with it. Most people are happy if you explain the situation and offer to meet later. That way you can finish your task and still help the other person. Often when you get back to the person who wanted to speak to you, you will find he or she has solved the problem themselves. It was just easier to start by shouting across the office to you.

Telephone interruptions In many ways these can be treated in exactly the same way as interruptions by people, though a ringing telephone can seem even more pressing and cut into what you are doing. Prioritize your calls. If it is high priority, deal with it immediately. Delay lower-priority calls until you have finished the task in hand by arranging to call back at an agreed time. It may be possible to delegate lower-priority calls.

Devise a route for paper:
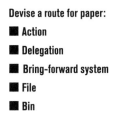
■ Action
■ Delegation
■ Bring-forward system
■ File
■ Bin

Develop Skills to Cope at Work

Writing a report

A report can be a major source of stress. The following tips may help:

- Start earlier.
- Develop a structure or format you can use each month.
- Use creative techniques, such as brainstorming, to come up with ideas.
- Keep the language simple.

Meetings

Planning a meeting can make it less stressful. For some people meetings represent a large part of their working time. Ensure that the time spent in meetings is effective and stressfree.

Identify the purpose of the meeting. Different types of meetings require different preparation, style of chairperson, and room layout. Decision-making meetings will be different from information sharings which may be different from meetings to generate creative ideas. Time invested in preparation will reap dividends later.

Circulate an agenda prior to a meeting. The items should be in a logical order and kept to the minimum required. Do not "blow air into" an agenda.

Environment The right environment is often not even noticed, but the wrong environment can destroy a meeting. Consider factors such as:

- room size
- room shape
- temperature
- furniture
- visual aids
- refreshments

Time Always plan how long the meeting will last. Tell everyone the projected time at the beginning, and try to stick to it.

Minutes Arrange for minutes of the meeting to be taken. This may include key action points or a detailed record of the discussion.

New technology

The introduction of new technology in the workplace is a source of stress for many people. If you are confused and frightened by the technology, don't be tempted to bury your head in the sand and hope it will go away.

Embrace technology. It is here to stay, so make it your friend. Ask for help if you are not sure about how things work; other people may be able to help you. Half an hour of help can reduce a lot of fear and stress.

Train, train, train. Ask to go to a seminar or request an interactive

Write to express rather than to impress

learning program. Most computer software is simpler to use than you think. Practice makes perfect! You will relieve a lot of stress by becoming familiar with computers and how to use them. You may also save a lot of time.

Chairing meetings

People are often put in charge of a meeting without any training or experience. The following tips may give you some support:

- Always start on time and have an agreed upon finish time.
- Clearly state the purpose of the meeting at the outset. Do not hesitate to remind others of the meeting objectives.
- Spend time agreeing on priorities at the start of the meeting.
- Don't allow a strong voice to drown out discussion.
- Identify likely points of disagreement.
- Natural adversaries should not be seated opposite one another.
- Always start the meeting on a positive note. It will help set the tone for the rest of the meeting.
- Listen well. Concentrate on what is said and the reactions to it.
- Summarize at the end of every item on the agenda and again at the end of the meeting. Everyone should leave knowing what has been decided.

Making a presentation

For many people this is one of the most daunting and stressful things they have to do at work. It is often the fear of giving the presentation – Will people listen? Will you make mistakes? – that is the most stressful, rather than the preparation or the actual presentation itself. Follow these guidelines to keep stress to a minimum:

- Prepare thoroughly, and don't leave preparation to the last minute.
- Know your audience. What is its knowledge level? What are the issues it is particularly interested in? What questions are people likely to ask?
- Practice before the actual presentation. If you can, practice in the room you are going to use for the presentation; this will help to reduce fear. Familiarize yourself with any equipment you need to use.
- Deep breathing before the presentation will help you to relax.
- Take your time and speak clearly. Make it easy for the audience to listen to what you have to say.
- Start with an impact. You only have a few seconds to create the right impression. Getting off to a good start will help you relax and gain the audience's attention.
- Even if you feel nervous, look as though you are enjoying the presentation. Smile!

Time Management

You may need to improve more general skills such as time management, assertiveness, goal setting and communication. By improving in these areas you can help to reduce stress in your personal life as well as at work.

Time management goes right to the center of life-planning and managing stress. It reaches beyond "to do" lists, leather planners and wall calendars. It is about what you want in your life and how you plan to achieve it. For many people the first challenge is "What do I want from life?" It is a very big question but an important one if you want to experience a sense of fulfillment. Take a few minutes to reflect on this, and then try to set yourself specific goals.

Prioritize

Many people base their priorities on urgency, but this means that often the quick and easy things are achieved at the expense of the larger, more difficult tasks that are really going to change our life. Priority should be determined both by urgency and importance.

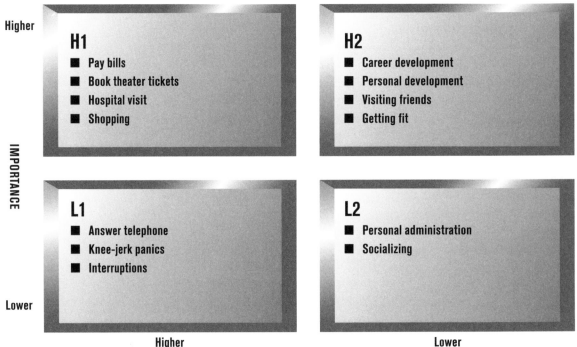

Higher

H1
- Pay bills
- Book theater tickets
- Hospital visit
- Shopping

H2
- Career development
- Personal development
- Visiting friends
- Getting fit

IMPORTANCE

L1
- Answer telephone
- Knee-jerk panics
- Interruptions

L2
- Personal administration
- Socializing

Lower

Higher   Lower

URGENCY

Make a list

Keep a "to do" list, and be sure to assign a priority to each of the tasks. Keep this simple, as in high, medium, or low. Your list will help you focus on the key areas of your work. If you don't prioritize your goals and tasks, it is human nature to do the things you enjoy or that can be done most easily. The longer, more onerous tasks get left until the end of the day or are carried forward until the next day.

Commit to start times

Once you have prioritized the task, give it a start time. Many people focus on deadlines. If you focus on deadlines, however, you may leave things until the last minute. Deadlines tend to act like magnets, drawing you towards them. If the deadline is Friday, all week you will be thinking, "I don't need to worry about this until Friday. I'll start the job tomorrow." Then, suddenly, it is Friday; and there is no more time left to meet the deadline.

Urgency and importance

Examine the table on the left. Many people become bound up in the activities that fall into areas H1 (high importance and high urgency) and L1 (lower importance and higher urgency), rarely finding time for H2 (high importance but low urgency). This can apply on a day-to-day basis or a more

To Do List	
Task	*Prepare for meeting on Friday p.m.*
Priority	*Medium*
Start Time	*9.00 tomorrow*
Deadline	*Friday a.m.*
Task	*Mail report to client*
Priority	*High*
Start Time	*Immediately*
Deadline	*Tomorrow morning*

life-changing basis. Ask yourself what percentage of your time you spend on H1 and L1 activities added together. To develop and live a really fulfilled life, what percentage of your time would you like to be spending on each?

Do you spend enough time on H2-type activities? These are the ones that are really going to change your life. What do you need to do more of to attain the right balance?

Most people don't plan to fail; they just fail to plan.

Time Management

Avoid procrastination

Procrastination is the art of convincing yourself that you can put off until tomorrow what you should be doing today. This applies to everyday things, such as repairing a leaking faucet or going to see the doctor, as well as to more personal development activites, such as gaining a qualification, starting a fitness program or looking for a new job.

The classic procrastination is when you are sitting at your desk looking at a piece of work thinking "The last thing I want to do now is this!" This is when you take a break, make a phone call, or visit the coffee machine. The problem is that when you return to your desk, the task is still sitting there. But now, instead of having one hour to complete it, you only have 45 minutes, or two days, rather than two weeks.

Identify the areas where you procrastinate, and act now to reduce panic and stress.

Plan your time

Having worked out your goals and priorities, successful planning will help you achieve them. Planning is the what, how, who, and when part of meeting your goals. Planning should be both creative and flexible – creative because you are planning into the future and the unknown, and flexible to help you cope with changes. Planning must have flexibility or it is useless.

Once you are fairly clear about your goals you need to work out two things: how much of your time and how far ahead, you can effectively plan. These will vary greatly from job to job. A person in a very reactive job, such as a nurse, may only be able to plan as little as a third of his or her time. Somebody in a less reactive job, such as a school teacher, can probably plan much more (perhaps a half) and further ahead.

In order to meet your goals you should plan in the short, medium, and long term. The short term for most of us is probably the next few days; it is the here and now and the culmination of all your other planning. The medium and

AVOID PROCRASTINATION

■ Be tough with yourself, and START those unpleasant tasks NOW.

■ When faced with a deadline, work back from it, commit yourself to a START TIME, and stick to it.

■ Break large projects down into manageable portions. That way you can deal with them a little at a time.

■ Have a clear idea of what the priorities are, and do the high-priority things first.

■ Do not allow yourself to be distracted by fun or urgent tasks at the expense of the high-priority tasks.

SHORT-TERM PLANNING – GETTING THE BEST FROM YOUR DAY

■ Work in synch with your own energy levels. Most people perform better in the morning than in the afternoon. Don't waste the morning on low-priority tasks.

■ Plan your day as far as possible, but leave room for the unexpected.

■ Give yourself 10 minutes of planning time at the start of every day.

■ Make a list of things you have to do. Prioritize these tasks, and give them a start time.

■ Avoid back-to-back meetings. They are guaranteed to create stress!

■ Batch your phone calls, and give yourself a period of "telephone time."

■ Use your planner to map out the day. Visual awareness will help you plan more effectively.

■ If you are required to read as part of your job, give yourself periods of reading time on a regular basis.

■ Always try to finish the day on a positive note.

■ Don't become a slave to your daily plan! It is only a guide and may require changing as the day goes on.

PROCRASTINATION IS THE THIEF OF TIME

It sneaks up on you, often when you are confronted with the following:

■ Difficult people/phone calls

■ Public contacts

■ Risky work

■ Unfamiliar work

■ Boring tasks

■ Large projects

long term will vary among individuals, and that is why it is important to have an idea of your effective planning time.

Medium-Term to Long-Term Planning

Identify your longer term goals. This will give you a sense of purpose and direction. Break larger goals down into manageable chunks, and use your imagination to work out the various possibilities and options.

Use a monthly or annual planning calendar to help. Visual awareness brings planning to life. Review your performance regularly, and modify your plans accordingly. Remain flexible in your planning, and don't be tempted to over-commit yourself.

Be Assertive to Stay in Control

Assertiveness is a mode of behavior that helps you to express your feelings, needs, and opinions, while respecting the feelings, needs, and opinions of the other person. It is based on the notion of rights. You have rights, and the other person also has rights. Behavior can be viewed as a range – from passive to aggressive. Somewhere in the middle of this continuum is a broad band of behavior called assertion. Using assertive behavior helps you to manage your response and reduce the stress caused by difficult situations.

Nonassertive people tend to grant all rights to other people and none to themselves. Aggressive people, however, tend to take all the rights for themselves and grant none at all to the other people they are dealing with. By contrast, assertive people actually recognize that everybody has rights and manage situations to recognize these rights.

SOME BELIEFS THAT LEAD TO AGGRESSIVE BEHAVIOR
■ Attack is the best form of defence.
■ Aggression gets results.
■ I am better than most.
■ Other people can't be trusted.
■ No one is going to stop me.
■ They have no rights.
■ Other people are stupid / ignorant / slow.

SOME BELIEFS THAT LEAD TO NON-ASSERTIVE BEHAVIOR
■ I am not very good at…
■ Other people won't like me if I say what I think.
■ My opinions are not as good as those of other people.
■ I can't.
■ I must be perfect.
■ I'll never be able to.
■ I wish I could.

SOME BELIEFS THAT LEAD TO ASSERTIVE BEHAVIOR
■ I have a right to express my opinion.
■ My opinions are valid.
■ I have a right to be treated with respect.
■ I am responsible for what happens to me; I am in control.
■ I can choose how I behave.
■ I can learn from feedback.
■ I have a right to make mistakes and will learn from them.
■ I have something to offer.

What is assertiveness?
Have you ever found yourself hesitating about raising an issue? Or once you have raised it being unsure about "how far to push it?" Perhaps you have been unsure of your ground, but blustered your way through nonetheless? You probably need to change your behavior to act more assertively. Assertiveness stems from mastery and adoption of principles in three areas:
■ What are the beliefs and habits that drive your behavior?
■ The words and phrases that you actually use.
■ The way you deliver those words and phrases – your body language.

Rights

Rights are important because they are one of the basics for deciding whether you or other people are behaving aggressively, passively or assertively towards each other. In a difficult situation, ask yourself:

- What are my rights?
- What are the other person's rights?
- Does the other person accept my rights?
- Do I accept the other person's rights?

In addition to rights expressed in law, there are less formal rights. Everyone has the right to:

- be treated decently
- express their views, beliefs, and opinions
- have time and resources to complete work tasks successfully
- say "no" without feeling guilty
- receive support from others so they can achieve their objectives

EVERYONE'S PERSONAL BILL OF RIGHTS

I HAVE THE RIGHT TO:

1 Set my own limits

2 Be treated with respect

3 Be listened to and taken seriously

4 Express my opinion, thoughts, and feelings appropriately

5 Ask for what I want

6 Make mistakes

7 Choose not to assert myself

8 Refuse requests or negotiate

9 Say "I don't know" without apology

10 Ask for time to think

Responsibilities

If you want to be seen as assertive rather than aggressive in standing up for your rights, it is crucial to accept the responsibilities that go with those rights. You must abide by the rules and conditions of your work and let others know when they have exceeded your limits. Treat others with respect; listen to them and take them seriously, recognize their right to express their views and feelings and to say "no."

Acknowledge your own mistakes, and do not be tempted to shift the blame to others. Put your mistakes right, and learn from them.

Give appropriate support to other people when you are able to; and be honest with your managers, colleagues and subordinates when asked.

Making Requests Assertively

The broken record

If you are trying to get a message across that the other person does not particularly want to listen to, use the "broken record" technique, which uses fewer words but to better effect. Use a short phrase or sentence to convey your request; and calmly repeat your request as often as necessary, using the same or different words. Slow down the pace of your speech, and emphasize any repeated words.

Do you sometimes find it difficult to make requests of other people at work? It is often easier to make demands of some people than of others. You might find it easier to ask a colleague than to ask a member of the staff or a superior. Typical requests might be asking a colleague for a report earlier than usual, asking a manager for a change of responsibilities, or asking a customer to do something different.

If you are not able to make requests assertively, you can end up missing opportunities, not taking initiatives and not getting the best use out of available resources. You might cause people to feel resentful and be uncooperative.

Remember, you have a right to make your wants known to others. Don't apologize or justify yourself for asking. For example, "I wouldn't normally ask but…" Resist the temptation to "oversell" your request with flattery or invented benefits.

Use assertive nonverbal behavior, such as a steady voice, good eye contact; and, if your request is refused, don't take it personally. The other person has the right to refuse.

Making requests

Decide what you think and feel. Be clear about your rights. Say what you want specifically and directly. Do not use verbal "padding" or make long-winded statements. Stick to your point, repeating it if necessary.

Acknowledge the other person's responses, but deflect comments which might undermine your assertive stance. Using statements starting with, "I know," "I recognize," "I appreciate," followed by a summary of what the person has said, shows that you have listened, even though you might not agree.

Refusing requests

A frequent source of stress is when you are faced with a request and find it difficult to say "no" or, perhaps when you do say "no," it comes across like a hammer blow. Any difficulties you may have often stem from the beliefs you hold.

- Others will feel angry or hurt if I refuse.
- They'll stop liking me.
- It's rude or selfish to refuse.
- If I refuse, I give up the right to make requests of others.
- Other people's needs are more important than mine.
- My needs are more important than theirs.

Remember that the other person has a right to ask, and you have a right to refuse. Set limits for yourself. In some situations you may not have the right to refuse, because of your employment contract. However, you still have the right to state any problems the request will cause you, and to try and negotiate an acceptable outcome.

If you do have to refuse a request, don't apologize profusely, justify yourself for refusing, or use excuses. Instead, use assertive nonverbal behavior, such as a steady voice and good eye contact.

Listen carefully to the request, and ask for more information if necessary so that you are clear about what the request will entail and the implications that agreeing will have for you and your team. Ask for more time to consider the request if you are not sure about your decision. Ask yourself, "Do I want to say yes or no? What is my gut reaction? Do I want to ask for more time to think about it?"

If, after consideration, your answer is no, make your refusal short and direct, but not abrupt; and incorporate the word "no." If necessary, use the broken record technique (left) to make it clear that you are refusing.

Once the refusal has been understood and accepted, it may be helpful to find out the other person's reactions to your refusal. If appropriate, you could offer an alternative course of action (but do not do so out of a feeling of guilt).

Bring definite closure to the interaction by either changing the subject or moving away.

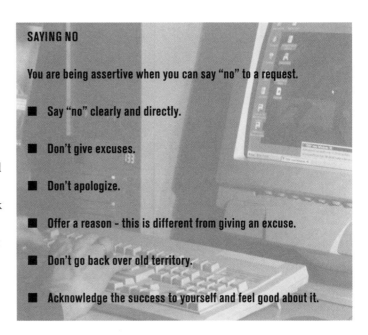

SAYING NO

You are being assertive when you can say "no" to a request.

■ Say "no" clearly and directly.

■ Don't give excuses.

■ Don't apologize.

■ Offer a reason - this is different from giving an excuse.

■ Don't go back over old territory.

■ Acknowledge the success to yourself and feel good about it.

Self-disclosure

Use the technique of self-disclosure to help you to manage your feelings at work. For example, if a late request for extra work from your boss makes you feel under pressure and intimidated, say so without becoming emotional. Being willing to express your opinions, feelings, and wants honestly and in a neutral way – where appropriate – is a crucial part of self-disclosure and assertiveness.

Unacknowledged feelings get stored up and can add to your stress level. They create ongoing resentment, which can eventually lead to an angry outburst or inappropriate reaction. Acknowledging your feelings, on the other hand, tends to decrease anxiety and stress.

Improving Communication Skills

COMMUNICATION

You communicate using your whole body in roughly these proportions:

■ body language 55%

■ tone of voice 38%

■ words we use 7%

Improving your interpersonal communication is crucial to building effective relationships with other people. Interpersonal communication is not confined to any single aspect of your life. You communicate every time you interact with other people. How effectively you do this ultimately determines the quality of your relationships and, when this affects your relationships at work, how successful you become.

Some people seem to be born with natural energy and confidence. Others have to work at developing it. You can improve your communication techniques and confidence by making a conscious effort to learn and apply new skills consistently.

THE FIRST 10 SECONDS

■ Walk into the room directly and without hesitation.

■ Introduce yourself by offering your hand to others and saying your name.

■ Maintain good eye contact.

■ Smile, remember the other person's name, and use it.

■ Have your head up and your shoulders relaxed.

■ Don't fidget with your hands or put them in your pockets.

■ Speak clearly, and don't be afraid to be the first to speak.

THE FIRST FOUR MINUTES

■ Be interested, not interesting.

■ Ask open questions ("Tell me...")

■ Take responsibility for introducing others you have just met.

■ Maintain confident body language.

■ Listen actively by using reflective/summarizing/clarifying statements. (For example, you might say, "So you're really enjoying your new job. What's the most interesting aspect of it?")

Solid eye contact

Look sincerely and steadily at the other person. When talking to an individual, maintain eye contact for 5–15 seconds. If you are in a group, aim to make eye contact with each person for about 5 seconds at a time. Do not allow your eyes to dart around, and do not overcompensate by blinking with exaggerated slowness.

Posture and movement

Stand tall, and relax so that you move naturally and easily. Stand erect, with your shoulders, hips, and feet in a line; and keep your energy moving forward.

Gestures and facial expression

Be relaxed and natural when you speak. The movements of your hands and arms are particularly important. Remember to smile if it is appropriate.

Dress and appearance

There is no right or wrong way to dress, but you need to feel comfortable and so does the other person. So attempt to dress in a manner that is appropriate to the environment.

Voice and vocal variety

Use your voice as an instrument. Carry energy and enthusiasm, and try to vary tone, pace, and volume.

You'll never get a second chance to make a good first impression

Language, pauses and non-words

Use appropriate and clear language for your listener with planned pauses. Be direct and positive avoiding jargon, fillers, and catch phrases.

First impressions

Within 10–15 seconds, we have made up our minds whether we like, trust, and are prepared to spend time with someone. If you create a negative impression, people will usually give you a few minutes and then turn their attention to other people.

Negotiating a mutually beneficial outcome can be a real test of your assertiveness and communication skills. Sometimes you may not have the right to refuse a request. You or the other person may not be able or willing to leave the decision as "no." You will probably need to consider and explore outcomes that are acceptable to both parties – a win/win outcome.

In order to work towards this you need to believe that your needs are as important as the other person's and that you do not necessarily have to lose for others to gain. When negotiating, use assertive nonverbal behavior, speak in a calm voice, and maintain eye contact.

THE VIRTUOUS CIRCLE

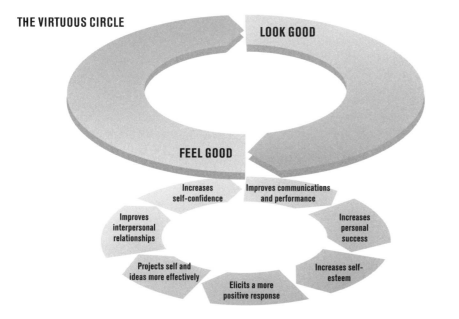

LOOK GOOD

FEEL GOOD

Increases self-confidence

Improves communications and performance

Improves interpersonal relationships

Increases personal success

Projects self and ideas more effectively

Increases self-esteem

Elicits a more positive response

Relaxation Exercise

Try this exercise to relax two or three times a week. Find a comfortable chair (not too soft). Make sure you have room to stretch.

Start to relax

Close your eyes and quiet your body and mind. Focus on different parts of your body.

Shoulders Lift your shoulders. When you feel the muscles really tense, hold the position for five seconds, and then release. Pull the shoulders down, hold for five seconds, and release. Now focus on the right arm. Bend the arm back at the elbow until the bicep feels tense, hold for five seconds, and release.

Right fist Clench your fist. Hold, then release. Stretch your fingers and thumbs out. Hold, then release.

Right leg Point your toes away from your body. Feel the thigh muscles. Stretch them. Hold, then release.
Bend the foot in at the ankle until the calf is tense. Hold, then release. Curl the toes and arch the foot. Hold, then release.

Left arm Repeat with the left arm.

Left leg Repeat with the left leg.

Buttocks Clench your muscles. Hold, and then release.

Abdomen Pull in the muscles as tightly as possible. Hold, then release.

Neck Tilt the head forward, feeling tension on the back of the neck. Hold, then release. Tilt the head to the left, feeling tension on the right. Hold, then release. Tilt the head to the right, feeling tension on the left. Hold, then release.

Face Clench your jaw as tightly as possible. Hold, then release. Smile broadly. Hold, then release. Close the eyes tightly. Hold, then release. Raise the eyebrows. Hold, then release.

Let your body relax. Be aware of your breathing. Aim for slow and shallow breaths from the abdomen. Think of a pleasant experience or event in your life that makes you feel good. Imagine yourself walking along the beach at the edge of the sea, water lapping around your ankles and your feet gently sinking in the sand with each step. The sun is shining. You are feeling warm and relaxed. Stay with that feeling and image for five minutes. Open your eyes and stretch. Spend a few quiet minutes simply enjoying the feeling of calm.

Breathing to Reduce Stress

Most of the time, breathing is an unconscious activity that we tend to take for granted. For certain activities and sports, controlling our breathing is crucial to effective performance. Swimmers, singers, and actors all spend vast amounts of time and a great deal of training to perfect their breathing. It can make the difference between a good and a bad performance.

Most of the time, though, we forget about how we breathe. This can lead to the development of bad breathing habits, which in turn can adversely affect the way we feel, both mentally and physically.

The next time you get a chance, watch someone breathing. Is the most noticeable movement from the chest and shoulders or from the abdomen? If he or she breathes from the chest and shoulders, that person is not making full use of lung capacity. Breathing from the abdomen is most effective and helps you to relax.

Calming breathing

This technique can be used in everday situations, such as interviews and meetings, to great effect. It can help you get through hectic periods of work or demanding times at home. By breathing calmly, you send a message to the brain

	Breathing Exercise
1	Sit in a comfortable but supportive chair – not a very soft one that you will sink into.
2	Let the chair support your back.
3	Drop your shoulders; feel them widen from the spine outward to the arms.
4	Allow your lungs and chest to expand fully.
5	Now take 5 slow, deep breaths, starting with an exhaled breath. Do not hold your breath. As you breathe in, your abdomen swells out slightly and, as you breathe out, it subsides again.
6	Continue by breathing in to a count of 1–2–3 and out to a count of 1–2–3–4.

that you are coping easily; the brain, in turn, sends signals to your physical body that you are calm and to stay that way.

Breathing exercises are among the most useful and popular relaxation techniques. They can be used unobtrusively in many situations. The more you use this method, the more you will begin to appreciate its effectiveness and reap its rewards.

Massage

Massage is another valuable aid to relaxation and stress reduction. It can help to reduce muscular tension and associated pain. Massage also stimulates circulation, speeds up the elimination of waste products by the body, and promotes a general feeling of wellbeing and relaxation. Touch can be used to relieve pain, to convey warmth and reassurance, and to energize.

Massage is much more widely used and accepted that ever before. While there are many trained, professional massage therapists, you can enjoy the benefits of massage by learning a few simple techniques. It is possible to massage yourself as a quick energizer when you are feeling tired, tense, or have a headache.

For the purpose of reducing stress, the most useful parts of the body to concentrate on are the neck, shoulders, and forehead. In the table below there are some quick massage exercises you can do yourself at work.

FOREHEAD

Sit in a relaxed position.
Place the fingertips of your left hand on your left eyebrow and the fingertips of your right hand on your right eyebrow. Using good pressure, slowly slide your fingertips outwards along each eyebrow until you reach the temples. Using small circular movements, massage this area. Bring fingertips back together, and repeat the process, working your way up the forehead until you reach the hairline.
Finally, spend a few minutes with your hands cupped over your eyes, with fingers resting on your forehead.

NECK AND SHOULDERS

Sit in a relaxed position. Place your right hand on your left shoulder. Using a "kneading" action, massage tense, "knotty" muscles in the neck and shoulder area. Repeat several times. Change arms and repeat on the other shoulder. Again, using opposite hands and shoulders, place your right hand on top of your left shoulder, and make small circluar movements with your fingertips on the back of your shoulder, working outward from the spine to the top of your arm. Repeat several times, then change arms, and repeat on the other shoulder.

Yoga

Yoga is a gentle exercise form that harmonizes the body and mind. It is now an increasingly popular way of relaxing and increases suppleness and vitality as well as reducing stress. True yoga is a complete system of physical and mental training. The foundation is having healthy eating habits; then comes the practice of physical postures and breathing techniques and, finally, meditation.

Practicing yoga

You can practice yoga at home, work, or in a class. Yoga is best learned from a professional who can help you with the mental control and concentration required. Once you have learned the basic techniques, it is possible to practice anywhere. If you practice regularly, your flexibility, strength, and breathing control will improve.

Yoga for beginners

Traditional yoga takes years of dedication to achieve a high level of mental, physical, and spiritual awareness. But it is possible to benefit from some simple principles and methods. By practicing daily you will feel more relaxed. If you think yoga could benefit you, try to fit it into your day.

Ten-Minute Yoga At Your Desk

1 Take a deep breath, and really let the breath go with a "whoosh." Clear your lungs.

2 Close your eyes, and spend 2 minutes doing the deep breathing exercise (page 69) to concentrate on your breathing and slow your body down.

3 Sit up in your chair, with the spine straight and feet flat on the floor. Enjoy the feeling of stability.

4 On an in-breath, stretch out your hands in front of you (don't hunch the shoulders). Really feel the stretch. Rotate the wrists one way and then the other for 15 seconds.

5 When you cannot stretch any further, interlock the fingers so that the back of your hands are facing you, and stretch upwards as far as possible. Enjoy the feeling. Gently release, and shake out the arms and hands.

6 Repeat the stretch upwards; but this time gently rotate the trunk from the hips to the left, keeping the hips facing forward. Breathe out and gently repeat, turning to the right. Do this three times on each side.

7 End by taking a few more deep breaths. Focus on the positive benefits and the energy throughout this brief yoga session.

8 Back to work!

5

Perceptions
Thoughts
Self-talk
Words

Is stress all in the mind?

Are my beliefs unrealistic?

Can I change my perceptions?

Is it all in the Mind?

**THE PROCESS CAN
BE SUMMARIZED**

■ A stress reaction is
something you create
in yourself.

■ It is your perception
of events, rather than the
events themselves, that
is the problem.

■ Believing that it is
the events that are
responsible keeps you in
the role of victim.

■ Only you are
responsible for your
reactions – emotional,
mental, and physical.

The demands upon you and your ability to cope may be real or perceived. Maintaining inner stability is also determined by how you choose to see things. Clearly, whether or not you experience stress depends partly on the how you see your circumstances. The "cause" of your stressful reactions is a combination of the situation you are in and the way you perceive it.

Anticipating negative outcomes

Most situations can be seen as neutral. It is only in matching the situations with past experience that we create a particular perception and meaning. For example, if the last time you were called in to talk to your boss, it was to be reprimanded, you will probably feel anxious the next time he or she makes an appointment to talk to you.

Not matching up to expectations

Situations take on significance when you try to force them to match your expectations and ideas of how things should be. If the reality does not match your expectation, this can result in conflict. By being inflexible, you are creating unnecessary stress for yourself.

Mental monologues

Your mental monologue is the constant conversation you are having with yourself in your mind. It goes well beyond the odd comment and phrase. These conversations tend to be negative, self-deprecating, and, ultimately, destructive.

Some people are negative by nature. If someone has a naturally negative outlook on life, a simple remark such as, "Lovely day, isn't it?" will probably be met by a negative reply such as, "Yes, but I'm sure it won't last."

Self-fulfilling prophecies

Mental monologues can be self-fulfilling prophecies. This means that if you think you will fail, you probably will. This can be comforting in one way. If you have constructed your "life script" around a negative feeling towards yourself or the world, it can be quite reassuring when something bad happens. If things turn out better than you expected or wanted, the negative-thinking person will probably dismiss it as a fluke. This is just one of the many mental games we play with ourselves, particularly when we are under stress.

Life positions

Mental monologues are a reflection of how you view life generally. There are four main life positions:

- I'm OK, you're OK.
- I'm OK, you're not OK.
- I'm not OK, you're OK.
- I'm not OK, you're not OK.

We decide these life positions, or they are imposed upon us, in childhood; and we tend to hang on to them for the rest of our lives. They become the center of our being and the basis for our mental monologues.

The last two positions are the most stressful because negativity is aimed inwards. How you react to praise illustrates the type of person you are. When an "I'm not OK, you're OK" person is praised, he or she discounts it and they will probably say, "It was easy," "It didn't need much sorting," or "Mary did all the real work." If you don't feel OK about yourself, you will certainly not feel worthy of praise.

How do you respond in such situations? What does it tell you about your life position? Is it helping or preventing you feeling good about yourself and other people?

How does your mind work?

Think of the conversation you have with yourself. How do you react to events and situations that put you under pressure? Is it a negative or positive monologue? Does it help you cope with the situation, or does it compound the problem? Is your mental monologue helping you through difficult situations or hindering you? Can you change it to put a better perspective on things?

If you are in the habit of negative monologues, think of some positive phrases that might help improve the situation and make it less stressful.

REAL OR IMAGINED STRESS?

Is there such as thing as a "real" cause of stress? Stress is subjective; it is personal. What causes one person acute anxiety may be a minor inconvenience to someone else. Do not fall into the trap of discounting your feelings by making comparisons with how someone else would react in the same situation. No matter whether the cause of your stress is external or internal, the effect is the same. You still need to take it seriously and take action to relieve the pressure.

Unrealistic Beliefs

Some of the beliefs you have about yourself, your role at work, and in life in general may be unrealistic and could be the cause of much stress.

Identify unrealistic beliefs

Assess your beliefs and how they make you live your life. Identify those that are unrealistic and also a source of stress, and start work on changing your perceptions. Remember, you are only a normal human being, not a super-human being. Be kind to yourself, and don't carry other people's burdens on your shoulders.

Do not exaggerate

Avoiding distorted thinking can help us see things in a different light and manage our stress levels. Avoid exaggerating the significance of a problem by using extreme words like "terrible," "awful," or "disastrous," when what we really mean is "inconvenient," "annoying," or a "nuisance."

Avoid "must," "should," and "have-to" words. When you hear yourself saying (or thinking) these words, change to "I would rather," "I would prefer."

A SCRIPT FOR LIFE
Many adults live their lives according to a "script" that has been written by somebody else. If you want to live a truly fulfilling life, take time to think about your own script for life!

Labeling can produce stress

Steer clear of labels such as "good" and "bad." Judging, criticizing, and moralizing tend to generate resentment, frustration, and self-righteous anger – all emotions that are counter-productive and create stress.

Avoid blaming yourself for something for which you were not entirely responsible. Always blaming other people and overlooking ways in which your own attitude and behavior might contribute to a problem also is not helpful to your self-development.

Early programming

Many of the unrealistic beliefs we carry in our minds stem from childhood experiences, good or bad. Childhood is the time when most of our internal programming takes place. It is during this period that we form and develop our belief systems, which stay with us for a long time. It is perhaps too easy to blame your parents for all of your problems, but the fact is that they did probably have the most influence on shaping you during your early, formative years.

It is important to identify and recognize the unrealistic beliefs you hold, and to try and analyze where or who they come from. You can then challenge their validity and, where necessary, change them to suit your more adult needs.

Nine Unrealistic Beliefs

1 It is necessary for an adult to be approved of by all significant others.

2 It is easier to avoid certain difficult situations in life than to face them.

3 I should be thoroughly competent, adequate, and achieve important things if I am to consider myself worthwhile.

4 I depend on others and need someone stronger than I am on whom to rely.

5 Unhappiness comes from external causes, and I have little or no ability to control my sorrows or disturbances.

6 My past history is an all-important determinant of my present behavior. Because something once strongly affected my life, it should have a similar effect forever.

7 If something is dangerous or fearsome I should be terribly concerned about it and should dwell on the possibility of it occurring.

8 I should become upset over other people's problems.

9 There is always a right, precise, and perfect solution to problems; and nothing else will do.

Case study

Jean was the youngest of four children. Her parents believed children should be "seen and not heard." As the youngest, she was always told to shut up as she knew nothing. Jean, now in her twenties, still remembers this. She is afraid to speak at meetings because she thinks nobody will listen to her. As a result, everybody talks over her; and all her good ideas are ignored. Jean now expects this; it's happened all her life!

Changing Perceptions

You can change your mind about the nature of the demands being placed upon you. You can change the way you think. Be supportive of yourself with thoughts such as:

- Perhaps it's not that bad after all.
- I've done more difficult things before.
- What's the worst thing likely to happen if I do this?

Positive self-talk

"Self-talk" is the endless monologue you carry inside your head. It has a great influence on the way you perceive things. Significant shifts of perspective can be achieved by reprogramming your self-talk. The messages you give yourself whenever you approach a situation and the mental picture you form of yourself before you attempt to do something are determined by your expectations based on past experience.

Self-talk can either be positive or negative. There are two ways of looking at the same situation. For example:

"This presentation is going to go well. I know my stuff and I can keep them interested."

"I am dreading this, everybody knows more than me, they will switch off."

CURRENT STRESSORS IN MY LIFE

Think about yourself in a positive way. What kind of self-talk do you engage in?

Write down something about yourself or your achievements that you are proud of.

What personal qualities helped you succeed?

I am proud of myself for:

SELF-TALK
The messages I give myself whenever I approach a situation

SELF-IMAGE
The mental picture I form of myself before I attempt to do something

PERFORMANCE
My behavior and performance is determined by my expectations based on past experience

Beware of negative thoughts

Unfortunately, many of us focus on the negatives. They can become powerful and block out the positives. Think of a recent situation you found stressful. What messages about yourself and your performance were going through your head? Were they helping you to be a winner or reinforcing your perceptions of yourself as a loser? Reflect on how you could have changed some of the words to help give yourself a more positive image about your performance. It is useful to keep a log of your negative thoughts and phrases and work on changing them.

When faced with a stressful situation, listen out for the negative messages you are giving yourself. Write them down, and turn them into positive messages. Repeat these to yourself. Make a list of your personal affirmations. Keep them relevant, sensible, achievable, and short. Don't aim to be perfect all the time, it isn't realistic.

Sporting wisdom

Sportsmen and women win or lose by their mental attitude. They spend a lot of time working on creating a positive, winning frame of mind. Top athletes have two kinds of coaches: the technical coach, who helps them swim faster or jump further, and the sports psychologist, who helps them create the winning frame of mind.

POSITIVE THOUGHTS ABOUT YOU AS A PERSON
I can cope.
I am OK.
I am as good as the next person.
I am willing to change.
I am loved by other people.
I can influence my destiny.
I am a good person.
I look good and feel good.
I enjoy my own company.
I can succeed.
I have triumphed over adversity in the past.

POSITIVE THINKING ABOUT SPECIFIC EVENTS
I will succeed in this presentation.
People will listen to me in this meeting.
I am nervous now, but I will relax into the event.
I can finish the report in time.
I can make a difference.
I have been promoted because I can succeed.
I can close this sale.
I can win this point.
I will achieve the results I want.

Olympic swimmers are not looking at the end of the pool, they know exactly how many strokes they take. They are looking beyond the pool to the image they have created in their minds of standing on the winners' podium, being presented with the gold medal. This image is what makes a winner. If it can work for them, it can work for you.

Thinking in a Different Way

SITUATION: FLAT TIRE ON A BUSINESS TRIP

Typical Mental Monologue	Constructive Self-Talk Alternative
"Damn this old car!" "I'll miss all my meetings." "It's hopeless."	"This is a bad time for a flat." "I'll call and cancel Jenkins at the next phone. I should make the rest of the appointments in time."

SITUATION: RECOVERING FROM A HEART ATTACK

Typical Mental Monologue	Constructive Self-Talk Alternative
"I almost died. I'll die soon." "I'll never be able to work again." "I'll never be able to play sports again."	"I didn't die. I made it through." "The doctor says I'll be able to get back to work soon." "I can keep active and gradually get back to most of my old sports."

SITUATION: TAKING ON EXTRA WORK WHILE A COLLEAGUE IS OFF SICK

Typical Mental Monologue	Constructive Self-Talk Alternative
"I'll never be able to fit it in with my own work." "How on earth will I cope?" "They expect me to do everything."	"I'll have to reassess how I organize my day and rethink my priorities." "What a great opportunity to find out what else goes on in the company." "This should help me bargain for a promotion and pay rise next year."

SITUATION: DIFFICULTY WITH A SUPERIOR AT WORK

Typical Mental Monologue	Constructive Self-Talk Alternative
"I hate that person!" "He makes me feel stupid." "We'll never get along."	"I don't feel comfortable with him around." "I let myself get on edge when he's around." "It will take some effort to get along."

SITUATION: ANTICIPATION OF A SEMINAR PRESENTATION OR PUBLIC ADDRESS

Typical Mental Monologue	Constructive Self-Talk Alternative
"What if I blow it?" "Nobody will laugh at the opening joke." "What if they ask about..?" "I hate talking to groups."	"This ought to be a challenge." "I'll take a deep breath and relax." "They'll enjoy it." "Each presentation goes a bit better."

SITUATION: DRIVING TO WORK ON A DAY YOU KNOW WILL BE FULL OF APPOINTMENTS AND POTENTIALLY STRESSFUL MEETINGS

Typical Mental Monologue	Constructive Self-Talk Alternative
"Oh brother, what a day this will be!" "It's going to be hell." "It'll never all get done." "It'll be exhausting."	"This looks like a busy day." "The day should be productive." "I'll get a lot accomplished today." "I'll earn a good night's rest today."

6

Diet
Relaxation
Exercise
Health

Can my diet help me to fight stress?

Does smoking help me to cope?

Is exercise a good way to fight stress?

Diet and Stress

Eating a healthy diet can help reduce stress. Eating well reduces stress by helping to maintain a healthy body. This means that your body is more capable of coping with the stresses you put on it. Eating well also prevents illnesses such as cancer, coronary heart disease, tooth decay, and obesity. What

you eat also affects your chances of suffering from high blood pressure and strokes, osteoporosis, diabetes, and other common illnesses.

Seven healthy steps

The World Health Organisation (WHO) recommends seven steps to healthy eating:

- Abundance
  Eat regularly and nutritiously.
- Satisfaction
  Include bread, potatoes, and cereals with every meal.
- Quality
  Choose lean meat, low-fat dairy products and all types of fish.
- Value
  Make healthy foods into good-value, delicious meals and snacks.
- Nourishment
  Keep consumption of fat, sugar, and salt to a minimum.
- Pleasure
  Enjoy the variety of healthy foods from all over the world.
- Choice
  Insist on healthy food as a consumer.

The WHO recommends eating a minimum of five portions of fruit and vegetables a day. Vegetables and fruit are high in fiber, vitamins, and minerals. For a stress-busting diet, eat vegetables, fruit, and salad with every meal. You can never eat enough of these foods. Try to

HOW HEALTHY ARE YOUR EATING HABITS?

- I regard eating, cooking, and food as a source of happiness.
- I take time for leisurely meals.
- I read and educate myself about nutrition.
- I eat a healthy breakfast.
- I eat three or more meals a day.
- I eat raw fruit and vegetables.
- I avoid processed and packaged foods.
- I am open to changes in my eating habits as I acquire new information.
- I am aware of the need for fiber and include enough in my diet.
- I maintain my recommended weight.

The more questions you answered with a "yes" the more healthy your eating habits and the better you are at managing stress.

eat bread, cereals, potatoes, and other starchy foods with every meal. (Potatoes are included with the cereal group because they are high in starch.) They are satisfying and full of nutrients. Whole-grain, starchy foods are a rich source of fatty acids, B vitamins, and minerals. Eat whole-grain breads and cereals that contain more fiber, vitamins, and minerals than white, refined versions.

Meat, fish, and dairy foods can be part of a healthy diet. Eat fish as often as you like and at least as often as you eat meat. Reduce the fat content of your diet.

Caffeine and stress

Caffeine, found in tea, coffee, cola drinks, and chocolate, makes body tissue more responsive to adrenaline. This can provide a temporary boost, but the negative results are:

- increased blood pressure
- change in the rhythm of the heart
- headaches / migraines

Slowly cut back over a couple of weeks. This will help avoid the withdrawal symptoms, such as headaches, fatigue, and depression that can result if you suddenly cut caffeine out of your diet.

Regulate your caffeine intake to two or three cups of regular coffee per day or six cups of tea per day. Use decaffeinated coffee instead and increase your daily intake of mineral water and fruit juices.

SOURCES OF CAFFEINE	
A cup of espresso	120 mg caffeine
A cup of cappuccino	120 mg caffeine
A cup of café latte	120 mg caffeine
A cup of filter coffee	103 mg caffeine
A cup of tea	80 mg caffeine
A cup of instant coffee	57 mg caffeine
Plain chocolate (100 grams)	43 mg caffeine
Can of cola	32 mg caffeine

Alcohol and stress

Moderate alcohol intake can be part of a healthy diet; but drinking to excess can cause depression, stress, and harmful physical effects, such as raising blood pressure. For a stress-busting diet, limit your alcohol consumption to 14 units per week (a unit is equivalent to half a pint of beer, a glass of wine, or a single measure of hard liquor).

Beware of business lunches

If you regularly do business over lunch, make sure that you are not over-indulging. Choose healthy options, and moderate your alcohol intake.

Skipping lunch or eating on the run is unhealthy. Make time for eating during the day and try to do it calmly. Lunch should be given appropriate priority. Not only is it healthy to eat regularly, it provides the chance to sit quietly and recharge your batteries.

Exercise

TIPS TO STAY WITH YOUR ROUTINE

- Train with a friend.
- Vary your workout.
- Choose activities you enjoy.
- Set yourself short, medium, and long-term goals.
- Vary your training.
- Keep your program short.
- Be patient.
- Be positive.
- Keep a record, and plot your progress.
- Reassess your goals regularly.

Regular exercise is a vital weapon against stress. As well as ensuring a strong heart and circulation, it is also an very good way to relieve tension. Regular exercise for a short period is better than the occasional long session. Aim to do at least 20 minutes of exercise a day, but any exercise is better than none at all. Most people have access to gyms, exercise classes, and parks, so there is no excuse!

Build exercise into your daily routine. Use stairs, not the elevator or escalator. Walk all of the way to work or; if that is not possible, take a bus or train for part of the trip and walk the rest. Buy the Sunday papers, rather than having them delivered to your door.

Maintaining exercise

When you get underway with your exercise program you will be enthusiastic. It is important to maintain that enthusiasm or you will become the next exercise drop-out. Vary the type of exercise you do to reduce the likelihood of becoming bored. Change the intensity, frequency, and duration of your exercise session.

Fit your exercise routine into your daily routine. For example, take your gym clothes to work with you.

Few of us can get by on self-motivation alone when it comes to exercising. Choose activities with built-in support, perhaps from a coach, instructor, exercise partner, or team.

ASSESS YOUR OWN LEVEL OF EXERCISE

- I generally try to climb stairs rather than use the elevator.
- My daily routine demands moderate physical effort (e.g. gardening).
- I include strenuous physical effort (e.g. construction work, laboring) in my day.
- I jog at least one mile twice a week (or equivalent).
- I regularly walk or ride a bike for exercise.
- I participate in a strenuous sport once a week.
- I do yoga or some form of stretching, limbering exercises for 15 to 20 minutes at least once a week.

If you have answered "no" more often than "yes", it is time to start exercising.

Rest and Relaxation

A hobby or interest can be a constructive way of relieving stress. Provided it is not too time-consuming, does not demand too much energy, or become a source of stress in itself, a hobby can provide a rich source of reward, pleasure, and recognition. Sometimes it can even "make up" for the absence of these feelings at work.

What hobby or interests would give an added dimension to your life? If you are very stressed, choose something that relaxes rather than stimulates.

If you lack mental stimulation, find something to exercise the brain. Creative writing, crossword puzzles, or charity work can get your brain working. If you want to meet people, joining a social group, trying amateur dramatics, or doing charity work are all good ways to make new friends.

A hobby that all the family can enjoy can be a useful way of spending more time together. Biking or visiting museums, for example, might be suitable activities to do together.

Relaxation

How often do you spend time relaxing? Just sitting doing nothing is not relaxing. Relaxation is a skill; and, like other skills it can be learned. It offers a way of switching off the sympathetic nervous system. Relaxation can induce feelings of

THE BENEFITS OF RELAXATION
- An easy way of reducing the stress response
- Increases self-awareness of the effects of stress on the body and mind
- Reduces fatigue by increasing awareness of excess muscle tension
- Increases confidence in one's ability to deal with feelings of anxiety, stress, and panic
- Techniques can be used unobtrusively in most situations
- Can improve personal relationships
- Promotes sleep
- Provides an alternative to drugs (prescribed and over the counter)

calm and wellbeing, while allowing you to remain in control and avoiding the harmful effects of drugs.

There is a wide variety of relaxation techniques, most of which are variations of a few basic methods. Physical relaxation techniques involve progressive muscular relaxation. Mind-relaxing skills call on the mind's imaginative ability. They usually involve focusing on a chosen object of contemplation or a series of pleasant and calming images, as used in visualization techniques, to eliminate distracting thoughts.

Some techniques call on both methods; but, whichever you choose, the basic principle is the same. Mental and physical tension go together; and, by relaxing the body, a feeling of calm and wellbeing can be induced.

Sleep Problems

Sleep is nature's way of allowing the body to recharge its batteries and prepare to face another day of stimulation, threats, challenges, and excitement. It is while you are asleep that your mind and body repair the damage that has been done to them during the day and that a balance is restored. When we are deprived of sleep, the physical and mental effects quickly become apparent. A lack of sleep will lead to physical exhaustion and a range of psychological effects, such as increased irritability and inability to concentrate.

Research has shown that, when it comes to sleep, quality rather than quantity appears to be the key issue. Stress is one of the main causes of sleep disturbance.

Disrupted and disturbed sleep patterns can be both a symptom and a cause of stress. Most people have lost sleep over their worries at some time – lying awake at night, trying to get to sleep while worrying about the present, and being anxious about the future. Failure to get a good night's sleep leaves us tired in the morning, bad tempered, slow to respond, and unable to concentrate. All are classic symptoms of stress.

Here are a few ideas to help you get a better night's sleep

■ Prepare yourself for bed with a slow winding-down process:
   - Take a warm bath
   - Enjoy a glass of milk
   - Go for short walk
   - Do not argue
   - Watch funny, light-hearted, or soothing TV, rather than disturbing news programs or horror movies
■ Learn a technique to help you switch off your mind. Sit up in bed, meditate for a few minutes first, and then lie down. Listen to relaxing music, or use aromatherapy oils in the bedroom.
■ Before going to bed, avoid caffeine, too much alcohol, or a heavy meal.
■ Set a routine sleeping time: go to bed at the same time each night, and rise at the same time each day.

INSOMNIA   !33

The main sleep problem is imsomnia – one in five people suffer from this inability to sleep. This may occur for short periods corresponding to a particular worry or stressful period. Normal sleep patterns should return when the worry is over. Some people spend a lifetime of not sleeping properly. It may also occur simply from going to bed before you are properly tired.

As well as not enough sleep, it is also possible to suffer from too much sleep. This causes the body and mind to slow down, and can create a feeling of mental fatigue, depression, and lack of energy.

Sleep is vital to our wellbeing and ability to cope with stressful situations. Few of us manage sleep effectively.

Smoking and Stress

Smoking is a harmful habit, which can give relief from stress in the very short term but will cost dearly in the long term.

When you are under pressure, smoking may make you feel better for a little while. It may seem to give you strength and to help you think more clearly. Smoking may also seem to help you socialize or speak more confidently. Although the relief that smoking appears to bring makes it a very attractive habit, do not lose sight of the gradual, long-term damage. Smoking may damage your health, your looks, your finances, and your relationships with friends and family.

Smoking is a negative reaction to stress, not a solution. Every day over 300 people die in the United States as a direct result of smoking. The best thing that you can do for yourself is to stop smoking now. Your self-esteem will rise, your bank balance will be healthier, and you will look and feel better.

You do not have to rely on your own willpower alone. Your doctor, voluntary organizations, and your friends and family are all around and are potential sources of help to you. There are also nicotine products on the market to help you to stop. These products aim to reduce some of the unpleasant withdrawal symptoms you might experience when you try to stop.

Ten-Point Action Plan

1 Choose a day. Will a weekend be easier than a weekday?

2 Get support. Tell family and friends that you are stopping. Ask them for their understanding and help.

3 The week before, start a list of all of the reasons why you want to stop smoking, and start to restrict the places where you smoke. Try not to smoke at home.

4 The day before, review your plan. Get rid of ashtrays and all lighters.

5 Reward yourself. Plan a healthy reward for the end of the first day, another for the end of the first week, and another for the end of the first month.

6 Have a plan. If it will help you to keep active, plan a busy first few days or weeks.

7 Think positively. There will be times when you will waver. Remember why you are stopping. If you are determined, the difficulties will evaporate.

8 Take this opportunity to make other positive changes in your life. This is the perfect time to start an exercise program.

9 Save the money that you would normally spend on cigarettes, and use it to buy yourself something special, such as a vacation or new clothes.

10 Take it one day at a time.

7

Identify needs
Develop skills
Action plan
Support

Where do I need to improve?

How can I develop my skills?

Do I need support?

Identify Your Development Needs

This section enables you to get the most out of the self-assessment you did in chapter two and helps you plan ways to improve your skills. You will identify areas where you should improve your skills, prioritize them, and make a personal development plan.

Watch yourself in action

The self-assessments in the previous chapters have given you an indication of the stressors and areas of your life you need to work on. Try to assess your own performance from day to day and week to week. Each time you are faced with a stressful situation or response, observe what reaction and feelings you have and how you respond. Record how it went; evaluate what was good and what could have been better. Think of practical things you can do next time to improve the situation. This doesn't have to be a major time-consuming exercise – just a few notes on a piece of paper or in your planner will do.

Where do I need to improve?

Compile a list of the attributes and qualities you feel are necessary to manage stress. Go back over your list, and put a star by the words you think already apply to you. Circle the ones you still need to work on.

Check out your characteristics

The list to the left gives some of the desirable characteristics you should be aiming to achieve when you are relaxed and handling pressure at work most effectively. How many of them match those starred on your list? People respond in a positive way to others who display these characteristics, so start to incorporate some into your daily pattern of behavior. You will be encouraged by the positive effects of handling pressure successfully and confidently and of adopting new behavior patterns.

Draw up a self-assessment table

In the table on the next page, transfer your ratings in the self-assessments in chapter two, listing skills as appropriate. Be honest when you complete the list. The exercise will also be more accurate if you get feedback from others. Ask them what they think of the way you cope with pressure.

How did you do?

You will have identified areas where you need to improve your skills and introduce strategies to reduce your stress. The next step is to produce a specific action plan. Repeat your assessment regularly in order to monitor your continued progress.

SKILLS	GOOD	SATISFACTORY	COULD BE BETTER
Dealing with complaints			
Maintaining concentration			
Using questions effectively			
Talking through problems and getting agreement			

Concentrate effort where it counts

Think about the areas of your job that you find stressful. Consider the helpful and unhelpful ways in which you react to certain stressors by examining them one by one.

Focus your attempts on improving the areas that have the greatest impact on you. Try to focus on the root cause of the problem, rather than on the immediate practical issues.

Stressful events list

Construct an event list to enable you to consider the aspects of your work that you find stressful. Analyze how you handle each one, what effect it has on you, and how you can improve.

To assure yourself that you have assessed your reaction correctly, ask a trusted colleague to check it for you. Can you identify areas where you can take practical steps towards improvement? Use this to develop specific action plans (next page).

EVENT LIST				
EVENT	WHO IS INVOLVED?	HOW DID I REACT?	HOW DID I FEEL?	AREA TO IMPROVE
MONTHLY MANAGEMENT MEETING	Managers and peers	Angrily when my team was accused of low performance figures	■ Picked on ■ Guilty ■ Annoyed with myself and the way I reacted	■ Listening ■ Controlling responses ■ Not always looking to blame others ■ Learning to say no to extra tasks

Development Action Plan

Try to lay out some benchmarks from which you will be able to judge how far you have progressed. Ask yourself, "How will I know if I am improving?" Also consider how you will maintain your higher performance level once you have improved.

Take each of the stressors you want to work on, and develop a detailed action plan. Do not try to work on several stressors at the same time. Pick one or two to start with. Make some progress on those, and then move on to the next. Some of the stressors may take long periods of time to change. If you want to change your job, you may need to retrain first. Just as companies have five-year plans, so can you.

Remember to set SMART goals. Break the actions down into manageable chunks. If the action is to delegate more, think about what you are going to

delegate and to whom. Don't leave it as a vague action "to delegate." The more you break it down, the easier it will be to do.

Focus on the benefits of making the change. This will give you something to aim for and motivate you. The benefits of getting a new job are that you will feel more challenged, your self-esteem will increase, and you will feel better as a person.

You may need help in tackling some of the stressors. Identify who can help you. Talk the issues through with them, and help them to realize why this is important to you.

Give yourself a review date. When you reach it, spend time reflecting on what has happened and how different you feel. If you have been successful, pat yourself on the back!

Mentors

Finding a mentor can help you to cope better with stress. A mentor is someone who works with you to give you support when you need it, helps you find solutions to problems, and offers the benefit of his or her experience.

Final word

This book is an ongoing aid to your development, so do not just leave it on the shelf once you have read it. The people who do well are those who continually improve.

ACTION PLAN

Stressor:

Development goals:

Benefits:

Actions by you:

Actions by your boss/the company:

Support?

To be completed/achieved by:

Index

If you liked Stress Management check out these career-building books from AMACOM.

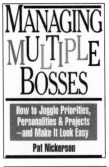

Managing Multiple Bosses
How to Juggle Priorities, Personalities & Projects—and Make It Look Easy
Pat Nickerson

"Pat provides specific potential solutions to 'real world' problems…Once learned and practiced, these tools can provide the opportunity to evolve from feeling like a victim to being in control of your own destiny."

—*Dick Nettell, Senior Vice President, Procurement Services, Bank of America*

$15.95   ISBN: 0-8144-7025-4

Shortcuts for Smart Managers
Checklists, Worksheets, and Action Plans for Managers With No Time to Waste
Lisa Davis

Shortcuts for Smart Managers provides fast and easy access to the key principles of 30 essential management topics, from budgets and business ethics to the fine points of dealing with difficult people, from mastering the Internet to planning an event, from negotiating and selling to strategic planning, and more.

$24.95   ISBN: 0-8144-0432-4

The Time Trap
The Classic Book on Time Management
Alec Mackenzie

From the hands-down authority on time management techniques, here is a completely updated edition of the national bestseller. *The Time Trap* is filled with smart tactics, hard-hitting interviews, and handy time management tools to help you squeeze the optimal efficiency—and satisfaction—out of your workday.

$17.95   ISBN 0-8144-7926-X

How to Resolve Conflicts at Work
A Take-Charge Assistant Book
Florence M. Stone

This how-to book not only helps assistants work well with others, but also shows how to work cooperatively and resolve conflict before it gets out of control. Included is practical advice on personality conflicts and operational problems, how to handle problem employees, building strong relationships, and much more.

$12.95   ISBN: 0-8144-7989-8

Call 1-800-262-9699 or order in your local bookstore.